"Vocational Interest and Visual Impairment Factors"

ABDUR RAHEEM

CONTENTS

Page Nos.

Contents
Abbreviations   ii - iii
     iv

Chapter Topics

    Page No.

1. **THEORETICAL FRAMEWORK**   1 – 23
   1.1 Blindness and Visual Impairment
        1.1.1 Blindness
        1.1.2 Visual Impairment
        1.1.3 Classification of Visual Impairment
        1.1.4 Terms related to Visual Impairment
   1.2 Vocational Interests
        1.2.1 Vocational Interests : Factors
        1.2.2 Vocational Interests: Role in Career Choices
   1.3 Socio-Economic Status
   1.4 Vocational Interest and Socio-Economic Status (SES)
   1.5 Study Habits
        1.5.1 Definition of Study Habits
        1.5.2 Effective Study Habits
   1.6 Statement of the Problem
   1.7 Operational Definitions of the Key Terms
   1.8 Rationale of the Study
   1.9 Objectives of the Study
   1.10 Hypotheses of the Study
   1.11 Delimitations of the Study

2. **Review of Related Literature**   24 -38
   2.1 Literature Review on Vocational Interest
   2.2 Review related to Study Habits
   2.3 Review related to Socio-Economic Status (SES)
   2.4 Research Gaps and Issues

3.	**Research Methodology and Design**	**39 - 47**

3.1 Description of the Variables under study

3.2 Population and Sample

3.3 Research Tools are used

3.4 Collection of Data

3.5 Statistical Techniques Used

4.	**Data Analysis, Interpretation and Discussion of Result**	**48 - 80**
5.	**Findings, Educational Implications and Suggestions**	**81 - 85**

5.1 Findings

5.2 Implications

5.3 Suggestions for Further Research

REFERENCES	**86 - 110**

Abbreviation

UN	=	United Nations
NSSO	=	National Sample Survey Organization
DGHS	=	Directorate General Health of Services
WHO	=	World Health Organization
VI	=	Vocational Interest
VPS	=	Vocational Preference Scale
SES	=	Socio-economic Status
SQ3R	=	Survey, Question, Read, Recite & Review
NIVH	=	National Institute for the Visually Handicapped
VET	=	Vocational and Educational training
ICT	=	Information and Communication Technology
ANOVA	=	Analysis of Variance
US	=	United States
CCCS	=	Comprehensive Career Choice Survey
APDI	=	Adolescents Personal Data Inventory
NARA	=	Neale Analysis of Reading Ability
TSHA	=	Test of Study habits and Attitudes
SESS	=	Socio-economic Status Scale
SPSS	=	Statistical Package for Social science
U.P.	=	Uttar Pradesh
SD	=	Standard Deviation
RTE	=	Right to Education (2009)
VPS	=	Vocational Preference Scale
Df	=	Degree of Freedom
f	=	Frequency
F test	=	Fisher Test
Sig.	=	Significant
AISES	=	All India School Education Survey
CISCE	=	Council of Indian School Certificate Examinations
NIOS	=	National Institute of Open Schooling

Chapter 1

THEORETICAL BACKGROUND

"The best and most beautiful things in the world cannot be seen or even touched. They must be felt within the heart."

-Helen Keller

Eyes are one of the most beautiful and prised organs in the human body used to view the world, so one has to face innumerable difficulties in the absence of vision. Childhood is a beautiful state of innocence and joy, but this is often not for children who are visually disabled. When they play and laugh, they feel isolated, as no one is beside them to hear or bear, as every day in their life is a big struggle. Disability is proven to be a big hindrance to the normal day to day life of visually impaired children. One hundred years ago, being visually impaired meant being condemned to a life of confinement and institutionalization. It was virtually unheard of that visually impaired people undertake steps to become educated and employed. Often seen as helpless by society and as a burden by the family, they could only dream of having a family and living an independent life.

As the years passed, many people have fought for our rights. They obdurately stood up for us so that today, persons like us (the blind and visually impaired) have the chance to live an independent life as freely as anybody else. The tasks of yesterday become the opportunities of today. As visually impaired people, we are taught to see life as a challenge; to face it, and fight for our independence. This means to be persistent in what is important to us: equality and non-discrimination. Through this ongoing fight, many changes such as improved accessibility technology, braille, and tools to help in daily living skills have aided us in showing the world that we can do the same things as anyone else. What was once supposed as a challenge has become an opportunity to demonstrate how far the visually impaired have advanced in today's society. Discrimination has always been a large challenge for a visually impaired person to overcome. It had never been easy but with the persistence of a few came the victory for many. Changes were made in our society because a few people refused to give up on something that meant so much to them. These changes have allowed the visually impaired person to become equal to the average citizen as opposed to a minor. It has allowed us to compete with our peers instead of being passed over for a job or a seat in a prominent college.

With new opportunities, however, comes the challenge that these opportunities are not fooled proof. With our technology comes a dependence on electricity, which is greater than anyone else and is limited to where we can access these technologies. It remains impossible for us to simply browse the books in a bookstore; the scanners needed to accomplish this are too large to transport for such a task. We need to face oncoming problems with the right attitude. Attitude is what has allowed us to meet challenges in the past and have them transformed into opportunities. Had Helen Keller not fought her way to higher education and freedom, many of us following her might not have the courage to stand up for our freedom and independence. Had Louis Braille not spent years developing the braille system, reading would still be a long and tedious chore.

The people of yesterday have lent a hand to shape our present and have given us the tools necessary to confront life with the necessary attitude to be successful. Thanks to them, we are no longer segregated and forced to live among our kind. We still have challenges daily. We must constantly deal with the pangs of discrimination and the injustices of those who fear us because we cannot see. Some researchers attempted to study socialization in visually impaired students and found that these children are considerably lacking skills related to social interactions (Movahedi A., et.al. 2011). The process of socialization is deeply affected by skills of daily living and it was found that visually impaired children had fewer interactions with friends and were rejected by sighted peers that lead to social isolation (Jones & Chiba, 1985). Adolescents with visual impairment seem to be socially more isolated, have few friends and small social networks, lack adequate social support (Anderson E.M. et al., 1982). Youths who lack social competence have been at risk for many difficulties including aggression, rejection, academic failure, loneliness, mental illness, and maintaining relations with others (Parker & Asher, 1987). Had it not been for those before us, however, many opportunities that we now enjoy would have been non-existent. The challenges of yesterday are the opportunities of today.

1.1 BLINDNESS AND VISUAL IMPAIRMENT:

Vision plays an important role in individual life. Visual impairment is a significant cause of developmental disability among children if the visual impairment is not treated or untreated it can have ample long-term inferences for the quality of the life of the child and the family and also can place the burden on the public health resources. The children having visual impairment also face lots of trouble with their education. Pupils should be able to look clearly and focusing on things farther and close by and be able to co-ordinate their arms and eye, differentiate small differences, and remember what they see. Difficulty in any of these things might present problems in the classroom. The perceptions and expectations that many people hold about blindness can have a significant negative effect on personal and social development (Scott, 1969). There is a tendency for parents of blind children to expect less or expect differences which may lead to lesser accomplishments and slower development of the child (Warren, 1984). Blind and visually impaired students are concerned about the limitations a visual impairment may impose on their career options (Heinze & Rotatori, 1986). Parents of blind and visually impaired children have many concerns about the future careers of their children (Jan, Freeman & Scott, 1977; Mc Callum, 1985). These concerns are well-founded as blind and visually impaired people have a chronically high rate of unemployment (Kirchner & Petersen, 1979; Miller 1992; Schmidt & Grace, 1989; Wolfe, Roessler & Schriner, 1992). They may experience discriminatory employment practices that inhibit normal advancement (Tuttle, 1984).

India in terms of the population occupied the second position in the world. The majority of the people live in the rural parts of this country with diverse social, cultural, geographical, and economic backgrounds. Visual Impairment or vision loss is one of the weighty social difficulties in our nation. Every year there are more than 2 million cases that cataracts persuaded blindness. According to WHO, there are over forty million people throughout the world whose vision is of poorer quality, 80%of who live in developing countries like India. 50 percent and above the blind population in the United States is over 65 years of age. It was estimated that 314 million people are visually impaired out of which 45 million of them are blind. Therefore, blindness is a global issue. An estimated 1.4 million blind children below age 15 will live in blindness for many years. Also, more than 12 million children ages 5-15 are visually impaired because of uncorrected refractive errors, the conditions that could be easily diagnosed and corrected with glasses, cataract lenses, or refractive surgery.

Directorate General of Health services (DGHS) and Ministry of Health & Family Welfare, New Delhi (2001 census) projected that there are 1.4 million blind children in the world, out of that 270000 blind children are in India and the prevalence rate is estimated to be 1.78%. The population of Karnataka is 5.20 crores. The incidence rate of blindness is 1.29 % (In 0-14 years of age group is 328 and 15-49 years is 2953) and the estimated prevalence rate of blindness is 16.7% per 1000 population and number of new visually impaired cases per year is 19, 386.

1.1.1 Blindness:

It is a condition where an individual suffers from any of the given symptoms, namely: Total absence of sight; or Visual acuity not exceeding 6/60 or 20/200 (Snellen) in the better eye even with correction; or a limitation of the field of vision subtending an angle of 20 degree or worse. For deciding the blindness, the visual acuity as well as field of vision has been considered.

Blind and visual disability is a great problem all over the world. The world health organization (WHO) (2002) estimates that for every five seconds someone goes blind. India is a home to World's largest number of blind people. 15 million (25%) blind people live in India out of 45 million blind people found to be present all over the World. Almost 5th of the world's visually impaired children live in India.

Loss of the visual acuity in children requires special attention. Visual impairment is an important cause of developmental disability among children, if these are undetected or untreated can have substantial long-term implications for the quality of the life of the child and the family and also can place the burden on public health resources. For evidence onchocerciasis (river visually impaired) is a serious public health problem with important socioeconomic consequences. The prevalence of on chocerceal skin lesions is unsightly and has a psychosocial effect on the affected person sighted adolescents; blind adolescents have a harder time with finding independence. They have to depend more on others to get where they want to go. Sighted adolescents can go off on their own. It is important for blind adolescents to feel independent. With the feeling of independence come a higher self-esteem and a better sense of identity. Blind adolescents those have high self-esteem and a strong sense of identity have an easier time adapting to their environments than those with low self-esteem and a weaker sense of identity.

The perceptions and expectations that many people hold about blindness can have a significant negative effect on personal and social development (Scott, 1969). There is a tendency for parents of blind children to expect less or expect differences which may lead to lesser accomplishments and slower development of the child (Warren, 1984). Overprotection, over assistance, denial and negative parental attitudes inhibit a visually impaired child's development of initiative, independence and realization of individual abilities (Cook-Clampert, 1981; McBroom, Tedder, Kang Ji, 1992; Warnke, 1993). Parent behaviour in areas such as childrearing, socialization of children, family structure and family interaction are also important to an individual's vocational development and subsequent career choices (Schulenberg, Vondracek & Crouter, 1984; Young, Friesen & Pearson, 1988). The development of self-concept has been associated with patterns of family interaction such as sharing of perspectives and challenges in a supportive environment (Grotevant & Cooper, 1985). Adolescent self-esteem has been linked to the quality of the parent-adolescent relationship as perceived by both parent and adolescent, as well as the control and reciprocal nature of parent-adolescent communication (Demo, Small & Savin-Williams, 1987; Walker & Greene, 1986). The family is a facilitator of experiences that expand or limit personal growth and also a primary source of knowledge about occupations (Grotevant, 1980). Parents provide a range of opportunities relative to their socioeconomic position such as educational and financial opportunities, role models and knowledge sources. The family and specifically the parents provide a reinforcement system of contingencies and expectations that subtly or directly shape work behaviour (Herr & Cramer, 1988). Parent expectations of children depend a great deal on their having access to information about career possibilities. The importance of parental and family influence on the vocational development of blind and visually impaired individuals is widely recognized (Graves, 1985; Rabbi & Croft, 1989). The consequences of positive and negative attitudes, expectations and adjustments are key issues in the career development of children with visual impairments (Heinze & Rotatori, 1986; Rogow, 1988; Warren, 1984).

1.1.2 Visual Impairment:

Visual impairment is a reduced ability to see up to a degree which creates problems not curable by usual methods. Some also include those who have a decreased ability to see because they do not have access to glasses or. Contact Lenses. Visual impairment is frequently defined as a best corrected visual acuity of worse than either 20/40 or 20/60. Blindness term is applied to complete or nearly complete vision loss. Visual impairment may cause people difficulties with normal daily activities such as driving, reading, socializing, and walking.

The most common causes of visual impairment globally are uncorrected refractive errors (43%), cataracts (33%), and glaucoma (2%). Refractive errors include near-sightedness, far-sightedness, presbyopia, and astigmatism. Cataracts are the most common cause of blindness. Other disorders that may cause visual problems include age-related macular degeneration, diabetic retinopathy, corneal clouding, childhood blindness, and a number of infections. Visual impairment can also be caused by problems in the brain due to stroke, premature birth, or trauma among others. These cases are known as cortical visual impairment. Screening for vision problems in children may improve future vision and educational achievement. Screening adults without symptoms is of uncertain benefit. Diagnosis is by an eye exam.

The World Health Organization (WHO) estimates that 80% of visual impairment is either preventable or curable with treatment. This includes cataracts, the infections river blindness and trachoma, glaucoma, diabetic retinopathy, uncorrected refractive errors, and some cases of childhood blindness. Many people with significant visual impairment benefit from vision rehabilitation, changes in their environment, and assistive devices. As of 2015 there were 940 million people with some degree of vision loss. 246 million had low vision and 39 million were blind. The majority of people with poor vision are in the developing world and are over the age of 50 years. Rates of visual impairment have decreased since the 1990s. Visual impairments have considerable economic costs both directly due to the cost of treatment and indirectly due to decreased ability to work.

1.1.3 Classification of Visual Impairment:

The definition of visual impairment is reduced vision not corrected by glasses or contact lenses. The World Health Organization uses the following classifications of visual impairment. When the vision in the better eye with best possible glasses correction is:

1. 20/30 to 20/60 : is considered mild vision loss, or near-normal vision
2. 20/70 to 20/160 : is considered moderate visual impairment, or moderate low vision
3. 20/200 to 20/400 : is considered severe visual impairment, or severe low vision
4. 20/500 to 20/1,000 : is considered profound visual impairment, or profound low vision
5. More than 20/1,000 : is considered near-total visual impairment, or near total blindness
6. No light perception (NLP) : is considered total visual impairment, or total blindness

Blindness is defined by the World Health Organization as vision in a person's best eye with best correction of less than 20/500 or a visual field of less than 10 degrees. This definition was set in 1972, and there is ongoing discussion as to whether it should be altered to officially include uncorrected refractive errors.

1.1.4 Terms related to Visual Impairment:

In defining visual impairment, three aspects of vision namely visual acuity, field of vision and visual functioning are considered simultaneously. In a broad sense, visual defects result into loss of clear vision, central vision or peripheral vision. All these losses are considered by measuring visual acuity, field of vision and level of visual functioning.

Visual Acuity:

It refers to the ability of the eye to see details. The visual acuity for distance is measured as the maximum distance at which person can see a certain object, divided by the maximum distance at which a person with normal eyesight can see the same object. Thus a visual acuity of 6/60 means that the person examined cannot see, at a distance of 6 meters, the object which a person with normal eyesight would be able to see at 60 meters. If vision is so impaired that to see the biggest E of the E-chart, the person has to come within 6 meters or even nearer, he is considered blind. The simplest method of testing visual acuity is to see whether the person can count fingers at a distance of six meters.

Field of Vision:

It refers to the field which both the eyes can easily see in the front. The normal field of vision is 180 degrees in front of eye. It is determined by the Confrontation Test in which mapping is done on a chart having concentric circles marked upon it. The simplest method of testing is to bring snapping finger from the side of the ear to the front, move it up and down, and mark the position where the person can see the finger.

Visual Functioning:

It relates in part to the condition of the eye. It is determined by the experience, motivation, needs and expectation of each individual in relation to whatever visual capacity is available to satisfy curiosity and accomplishment activities for personal satisfaction. The visual functioning refers to the degree to which/ability of a person to use vision for all (daily) activities.

1.2 VOCATIONAL INTERESTS:

Vocational interest have been defined by different workers in the field. Bingham explain that Vocational Interest are a sort of attitude through which an individual does an action when he gets the opportunity. Forer (1953) went on to describe the vocational interests in terms of emotional and personal requirements. Holland (1959) renders a kind of personality trait explanation to the vocational interests. Holton (1962) searches vocational interests as reduction in the needs tension. While on the otherside, Hollingshead speaks of vocational interests in respect of the individuals socio economic status. Roe (1956) opined concerning the vocational preferences upon the base of wants, family, avoidance, acceptance, and emotion concentration. Around the age of 17 and 18 years, it has been observed that the vocational interests become nearly stable (Abraham, Pant, Amit, and Rashmi, 2004). Though generally, the students select a profession choice that is largely popular around them and pursue the courses which are acceptable socially and furthermore which have a certain amount of status attached with them in the society around them. As a result of these prestige requirements or needs there is found a wide range of variability in the occupational preferences of pupils as the status matters are different in every cultures and distinct regions of the nation and between the persons belonging to varied socio economic status levels. Accordingly, some people like the administrative professions while on the other hand others may like to graduate as doctors, engineers or lawyers.

1.2.1 Vocational Interests: factors

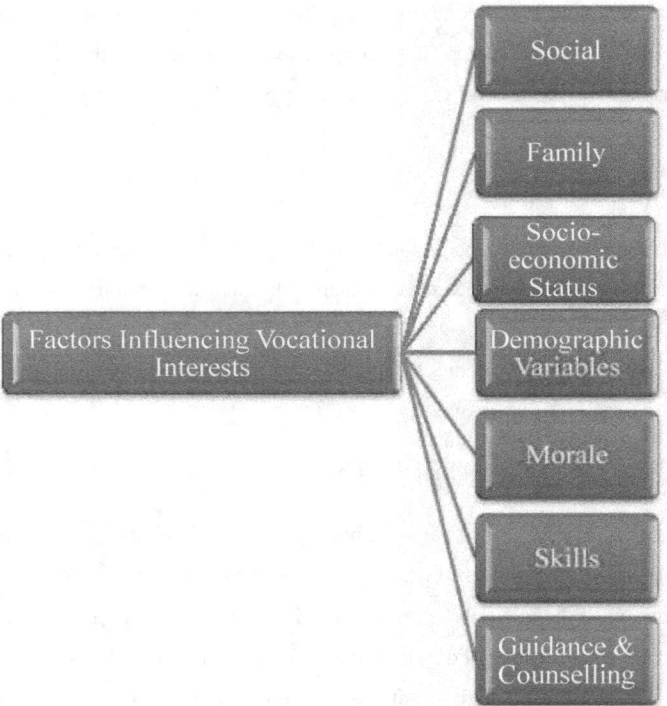

Figure 1 Factors that affect the vocational interests.

1. **Social Factors**

Persons aspire for the vocational courses that they see prevalent in the society. Certain vocation that may be considered better in the society can appear to be interesting to the students else they might get attracted to distinct other professions which they find around themselves in the society such as doctors, engineers, pilots etc. The income of a person plays a essential role in ascertaining what type of school he attends and that would have effect on the type of qualification.

2. Familial Factors

Individual have occupational interests inspired from their family members. If anybody in the family is a lawyer children also want to be a lawyer. In India the career planning is generally done by parents (Bhargava and Arora, 2004). The aspirations of the parents have a great effect on the vocational interests of students (Caplow, 1954).

3. Socio Economic Status

This is a very important factor influencing the occupational interests of pupils. For example a student hailing from lower socio economic level group may desire to get work early and do a diploma or other vocational or technical course. While a student belonging to a high socio- economic level family can study up to higher level.

4. Demographic Variables

Demographic variables like gender and age also affect the vocational interests of students to a large extent. Generally girls aspire to be doctors whilst boys show an inclination towards the technical profession.

5. Morale

Morale of a person also lends a significant contribution in the selection of a good career (Raina and Bhargava, 2002). Low or high morale affects the vocational interests. A person who is confident about his or her capabilities may like a high demanding vocation and a person with a low morale may choose a low demanding career.

6. Skills

These determine a student's vocational interests. Pupil having mathematical skills can become an engineer while student skills for the art subjects may become a civil servant. Providing vocational training to students according to their skills and interests is a scientific process (Bhargava, 1994).

7. **Guidance and Counselling**

Students go for opting for their careers by availing some sort of counselling service. Guidance and counselling services assist the pupils a long way in selecting appropriate careers. The career guidance and counselling are very essential for deciding vocations (Zunker, 1994).

1.2.3 Vocational Interests: Role in Career Choices

Vocational interests go to play a leading role in the career decision of pupils. Holland says that, individuals who prefer to work in the environments similar to their personality types will be more likely to be successful. Career options selected by the students depends on the type of Vocational interests they have as is established by various researches.

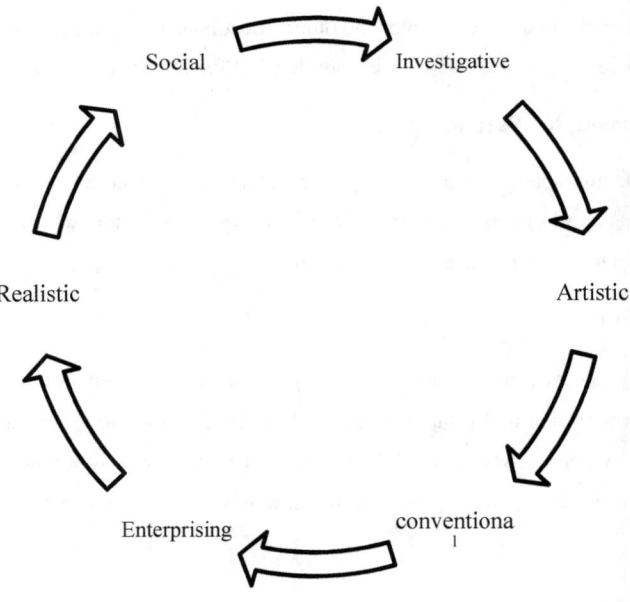

Figure 1.9 Holland's Taxonomy of Vocational Interests

1.3 SOCIO ECONOMIC STATUS:

The socio economic status has been defined by the social scientists as the relative position of a person in the society based on income, power, and background.

The significant variables that are employed most frequently by the social scientists as regards to measuring the socio-economic status are income, education, and occupation.

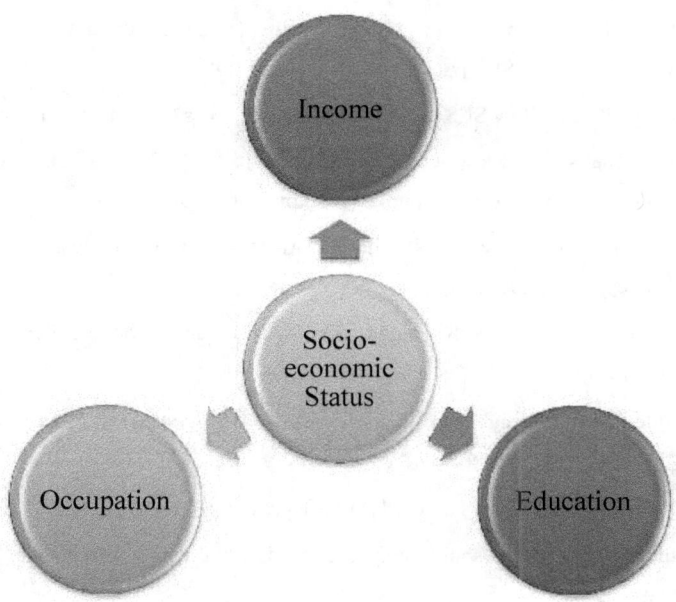

Fig. 1.10 Attributes of Socio-economic Status.

An explanation of these is given here-

i) **Income**: What an individual earns is termed as his or her income. Salary and savings come under its purview. The wealth and immovable assets also come in the heading of income.

ii) **Education**: The income is influenced by the status of educational attainment of an individual. Income increases with education along with an enhancing of socio economic status.

iii) **Occupation:** People engaged in higher level occupations as lawyers and engineers have higher incomes than people employed in lower occupations and thus have higher socio economic status.

1.4 VOCATIONAL INTEREST AND SOCIO-ECONOMIC STATUS (SES):

Many researchers have studied the relation between Vocational interests and socio-economic status. Some of them are listed below-

1. The skills of low socio economic status (SES) pupils develop slowly as compared to high SES pupils (Morgan, et. al., 2009).
2. The institutes in low SES areas are low on resources (Arkens, Barbarian, 2008).
3. Vocational skills of low social economic status students are low as compared to high socio economic status pupils (Buckingham, et.al., 2013).
4. Low socio economic status children have lesser access to learning resources (Bradley, et.al., 2001).
5. Students from low SES groups lack in information about college resources (Brown, et.al., 2016).
6. Students from higher SES schools have higher vocational aspirations (Chaudhry, et.al., 1998).
7. Career choices for boys and girls are affected by SES (Arora, 1988).
8. Students from high socio economic levels obtain high percentage (Chandra, et.al., 1990).
9. Vocational aspirations and SES had significant relationship (Dabir, O, 1986).
10. Social and economic status had significant relationship with occupational aspirations (Mathur, et.al., 1984).

1.5 STUDY HABITS:

It was believed by various investors of education that study habits and attitudes have a considerable effect on academic achievement of the students. This is true at every level of education, but more specifically in secondary school level where much emphasis is given on academic achievement. Also, it may be considered that good academic achievements are result of good study habits. Before discussing which factors of study habits contribute much in developing desired study habits and why study habits need to be discussed? It would be better to discuss the term "study". Sometimes learning and study are used interchangeably; however there is some difference in between the two terms (Burns & Dobson, 1984). Oxford dictionary defines learning as "knowledge got by study; to get knowledge by study". It implies that learning is the end product of study. 'Study' is defined as "devotion of time and thought that to acquiring information; pursuit of some branch of knowledge". Consequently, study is not a static process rather it is an active process by which learning is acquired. Students engage themselves in study due to numerous reasons viz. to quench the thirst of knowledge; to secure the future; to please parents, teachers and peers of opposite sex; to avoid punishment, etc. Oxford dictionary defined the 'habit' as "a settled or higher tendency or practice, especially one that is hard to give up". The process of study is developed by inner-self of a student and it must be activated. It has been mentioned above that "good academic achievers have good study habits without taking pressure; these are the students who value isolation and independence in the study environment" (Burns & Dobson, 1984, p700). Teacher acts as a resource in the teaching learning process. However, the task of learning is not solely dependent on teachers. It is not the only teacher's responsibility but also of the learner's responsibility simultaneously. Efficient learning depends not only on good teaching but also on satisfactory learning procedures. Efficient learning depends on learner's ability to schedule his time, the plan of his study, the habit of concentration, note taking, mental review, the judicious application of whole and part methods, massed and distributed learning and so on. In other words learning involves the development of Study Habits. Many reading reforms have been formulated in the education system of India, but no stress has been given on developing desired study habits in pupils. The most important requisite for effective study is a good system of study. In present system, more stress is laid on academic performance of the students but a good academic achievement is not possible without good Study Habits. Thus, study habits are true indicators of individuality of a person. These are planned programme of subject mastery. They characterize the learner's learning character. In fact, every learner has a peculiar method of style of pursuing his or her academic tasks. These Study Habits also serve as the vehicle of learning. The problem of Study habit is of immense important both from the theoretical and practical points of view. When we work at the theoretical point of view, development of efficient Study Habits and skill forms the basis of efficient learning and as such one of the continuous objectives of teaching should be the inculcation of good study habits and skills amongst the students. From the practical point of view, the problem is more important. Often the teachers come across such students whose behaviour show average scholastic aptitude, yet they perform very poorly in their courses of study. A large majority of these seem to have faulty Study Habits. Proper guidance would help them to change their faulty study habits into desirable ones. Psychologists agree that the physical and material aspect that imbibes in students a sense of dedication to learning which we may call it as a study habit can also be an important outcome of academic climate. When the environmental conditions are radically altered, significant changes occur in developing good study habits among the students, which cumulatively brings an elevated academic achievement.

1.5.1 Definition of Study Habits:

Different definitions of study habits are listed below as given by various sources-

1. Chadha (2006) stated that the independent learning skill was required for those secondary students going on to college and also into the ever changing workplace.

2. Weiner, in 1995, (as cited by Tuckman) emphasized "the student takes responsibility" method of teaching in which the student realized how their efforts affected their test grade.

3. Tuckman (2003) defined study skills as "the learning and motivation strategies that enable a student to be successful".

4. Good (1973) defined the term Study Habit as "the student's way of study whether systematic, efficient or inefficient, etc." Good Study Habits are perceived to be the determinants of the academic performance that is why efforts are made to develop an improved study habits in students. Study habits refer to the activities carried out by learners during the learning process of improving learning. Study habits are intended to elicit and guide one's cognitive processes during learning.

5. Patel (1976) defined study habits include home environment & planning of work, reading & note taking habits, planning of subjects, habits of concentration, preparation for examination, general habits & attitudes, school environment.

6. Thoday (1957) reported a "fairly clear relationship between examination results and the amount of work done",

7. Malleso working on the assumption that students would find difficulty in reporting their activities accurately,

8. Entwistle and Entwistle (1970) provided a specially designed grid from which "hours worked" could be derived. Using this grid method, consistently significant relationships with degree results have subsequently been reported.

9. Another pattern of study behaviour which involves unconscious conflict has been described by Blaine and McArthur (1971). Here the student has a desperate need for autonomy in his studying, rejecting pressures to conform to conventional academic requirements.

10. Arora, 1973 defined Study habit as the tendency of a pupil to study when the opportunities are given, the pupil's way of studying whether systematic or unsystematic, efficient or inefficient etc.

1.5.2. Effective Study Habits

Effective study habits are the habits that should be practiced in order to improve the learning. It is not enough to simply think about studying as it does not guarantee better results; one has to actually practice it, and in the process use information to get better results. This is the chief idea of this section and this section completely depends on this concept. There is a general saying that practice doesn't make perfect, perfect practice makes perfect. Following are the main points that need to be remembered for adopting the good study habit. Before one even starts to think about the process of studying, one must develop a schedule. Without a proper schedule or plan for studying one can not allocate the valuable time when unannounced situation arises. A well planned schedule can prove to be a lifesaver in unforeseen situations. It's up to the learner to develop a schedule that meets requirements of the learner; revise it if necessary and most essential to follow it. A good schedule saves time and energy. One thing everyone should consider that it should be planned with the idea that it can be revised if needed. A good schedule keeps the learner from wandering off the syllabus. A good schedule, if properly managed, assigns time where time is needed also avoids the wasting of time. A schedule should take into account every class, laboratory, lecture, social event, and other work in which a learner has to engage himself. There are engagements such as classes, play time, exercise time, leisure time, etc. that has to be incorporated in the schedule. One must focus on the leisure time available and how the learner uses it wisely. Learner should make a weekly schedule and block off the twenty-four hours day in one hour increments. Indicate times for classes, labs, lectures, social, and work time. Also assign a period for sleeping or taking rest to reenergize again. This gives the student a rough road map of the time available. Of course, there is a room to revise the schedule as need arises. The problem of when to study is also vital. Study should be carried out only when learner has taken a rest, and is prepared, and also has planned for it. Last minute studying just before an examination or class is usually a waste of time. It does only mugging up the content and consequently does not imbibe learning. If a learner is planning to study before a lecture or class, learner must read all the assignments and make notes on the tougher topics which seem to have importance in examination. If the learner studies after the lecture or class then it is better to review the notes taken during class while the information is still fresh. For classes that require recitation, such as foreign languages, learner should practice the content just before the class. Use the time wisely to practice. Sometimes, practice with peers can help sharpen the skills in a before class study period. Learner should not be afraid to revise the schedule. Schedules are real plans for using the time. If a schedule doesn't works, revise it. Learner must understand that schedule helps to develop good study habits. Once the learner cultivates good study habits schedule building becomes easier which enhances learning. Time is the most valuable resource in a student's life. In spite of that, it is also one of the most wasted resources. The schedule you developed should guide you in how to allocate the available time in the most productive manner. Sticking to the schedule can be tough. It is not advisable to waste away valuable time. Simply avoiding study is the easiest job in the world. I am up to the learner to stick to the schedule. A good deal of success in secondary school stage or college depends on this simple truth. Learning can be done anywhere. One important method of reading is SQ3R method. SQRRR or SQ3R is a reading comprehension method named for its five steps-

a) Survey,
b) Question,
c) Read,
d) Recite, And
e) Review.

a) Survey:

The first step, survey or skim, advises that one should resist the temptation to read the book and instead first go through a chapter and note obviously, some places are better than others. Libraries, study lounges or private rooms are best. Above all, the place chosen to study should not be distracting. However, distractions can be built up anywhere. Choosing a good physical environment is must be a part of study habits. It was introduced by Francis P. Robinson, an American education philosopher in his book Effective Study" in 1946. The method offers a more efficient and active approach to reading textbook material. It was created for college students, but is extremely useful for young students as well. Classrooms all over the world have begun using this method to better understand what they are reading. Everybody has thinking skills but only few of them use them effectively. Effective thinking skills can't be studied, but can be built-up over a period of time through experiences, knowledge and wisdom. Good thinkers sometimes foresee a possibility whereas others see a dead end situation. If a learner has to achieve this level of thinking skills, he should think everything rationally and critically. Discussing with peer group, teachers and elders can be beneficial in acquiring of good thinking skills. This survey step only takes 3-5 minutes, but it provides an outline or framework for what will be presented. The learner should identify the ideas present in the text and formulate questions about the content.

b) Question:

Second step of this method is to generate questions about the content of the reading. For example, convert headings and sub-headings into questions, and then look for answers in the content of the text. Other more general questions may also be formulated such as, what is the central idea of the content? How does it help me?

What is the author trying to say? The Question step again only takes 3-5 minutes to complete, but it will motivate the reader to seek answers to the questions.

c) **Read (R1):**

Use the background work done with 'S' and 'Q' in order to begin reading actively. This means reading in order to answer the questions raised under 'Q'. Passive reading, in contrast, results in merely reading without engaging with the study material.

d) **Recite (R2):**

The second 'R' refers to the part known as recite. The learner should try to retrieve from memory what was learned in the same manner as telling someone else about the information. It is important that the reader use his/her own words in order to formulate and conceptualize the material. Try recalling and identifying major points and answers to questions from the 'Q' step. This recital step may be done either in an oral or written format and is related to the benefits of retrieval (testing effect) in boosting long-term memory for the material.

e) **Review (R3):**

The final 'R' is review. Once learner reaches the end of the passage, he should say back to himself what the point of the whole passage is. Again using own words.

1.6 STATEMENT OF THE PROBLEM:

The investigator selected the problem for the present study is formally stated as:

"A study of vocational interest among visually challenged adolescents in relation to certain personal, familial and demographic variables."

1.7 OPERATIONAL DEFINITIONS OF THE KEY TERMS:

Vocational Interest:

The preferences shown by the pupils in selecting certain career choices is called their vocational interests.

Socio-economic Status:

It is an economic and sociological measure of a person's work experience and an individual's or family's economic level.

Study Habits:

These are learned patterns of studying that may occur with or without conscious awareness or deliberate efforts.

Gender:

It is the sexual identity of the students, i.e. Male and female senior secondary students.

1.8 RATIONALE OF THE STUDY:

Adolescence is the age of physical changes, psychological development, and social adjustment. Growth and development occur in interaction with other people that are important to adolescents such as parents, siblings, relatives, friends, and school personnel. The period of adolescence may cause a great deal of anxiety for the persons with a physical handicap, who faces not only the usual developmental challenges but also the added strain of his or her physical handicap. Visually challenged adolescents have problems in their relationship with friends such as social isolation, being rejected by their peers, having fewer friends, lower socioeconomic status. The visual impairment also interferes with the adolescent's social relationship with friends and social activities. They also spend more time alone in passive activities. The present study is substantial as it is going to explore the vocational interests, study habits and socioeconomic status (SES) of visually challenged adolescents. The vocational needs of the visually challenged adolescents can be brought to light and the required steps are initiated to meet those vocational needs. On account of all these reasons, the investigator wishes to conduct this study to acquire information concerning vocational interest of visually challenged adolescents in relation to their study habits and socioeconomic status.

1.9 OBJECTIVES OF THE STUDY:

1. To ascertain the significance relationship between vocational interest and study habits (personal variable) among visually challenged adolescents.

1.1. To ascertain the significance relationship between high vocational interest and high-level study habits (personal variable) among visually challenged adolescents.

1.2. To ascertain the significance relationship between low vocational interest and low-level study habits (personal variable) among visually challenged adolescents.

2. To ascertain the significance relationship between vocational interest and socio-economic status (familial variable) among visually challenged adolescents.

2.1. To ascertain the significance relationship between high vocational interest and high-level socio-economic status (familial variable) among visually challenged adolescents.

2.2. To ascertain the significance relationship between low vocational interest and low-level socio-economic status (familial variable) among visually challenged adolescents.

3. To ascertain the individual and combined effect of study habit and socio-economic status on vocational interest of visually challenged adolescents.

3.1. To ascertain the individual and combined effect of high-level study habit and high-level socio-economic status on high vocational interest of visually challenged adolescents.

3.2. To ascertain the individual and combined effect of low-level study habit and low-level socio-economic status on low vocational interest of visually challenged adolescents.

4. To compare vocational interest between male and female visually challenged adolescents.

5. To compare vocational interest between rural and urban visually challenged adolescents.

6. To compare study habit between male and female visually challenged adolescents.

7. To compare study habit between rural and urban visually challenged adolescents.
8. To compare socio-economic status between male and female visually challenged adolescents.
9. To compare socio-economic status between rural and urban visually challenged adolescents.

1.10 HYPOTHESES OF THE STUDY:

1. There is no significance relationship between vocational interest and study habits (personal variable) among visually challenged adolescents.
1.1. There is no significance relationship between high vocational interest and high-level study habits (personal variable) among visually challenged adolescents.
1.2. There is no significance relationship between low vocational interest and low-level study habits (personal variable) among visually challenged adolescents.
2. There is no significance relationship between vocational interest and socio-economic status (familial variable) among visually challenged adolescents.
2.1. There is no significance relationship between high vocational interest and high-level socio-economic status (familial variable) among visually challenged adolescents.
2.2. There is no significance relationship between low vocational interest and low-level socio-economic status (familial variable) among visually challenged adolescents.
3. There is no individual and combined effect of study habit and socio-economic status on vocational interest of visually challenged adolescents.
3.1. There is no individual and combined effect of high-level study habit and high-level socio-economic status on high vocational interest of visually challenged adolescents.
3.2. There is no individual and combined effect of low-level study habit and low-level socio-economic status on low vocational interest of visually challenged adolescents.

4. There is no significance difference in vocational interest between male and female visually challenged adolescents.

5. There is no significance difference in vocational interest between rural and urban visually challenged adolescents.

6. There is no significance difference in study habit between male and female visually challenged adolescents.

7. There is no significance difference in study habit between rural and urban visually challenged adolescents.

8. There is no significance difference in socio-economic status between male and female visually challenged adolescents.

9. There is no significance difference in socio-economic status between rural and urban visually challenged adolescents.

1.11 DELIMITATIONS OF THE STUDY:

1. The research was carried out in selected schools, i.e. Ahmadi School for the Blind, Aligarh and National Institute for the visually handicapped (NIVH), Dehradun. Thus, its generalizations may not be extended beyond Aligarh and Dehradun.

2. Vocational Interest has been studied in relation to only two variables, Study Habits and Socio-economic Status.

3. The present study is focused only on visually challenged adolescents, And thus, does not cover the entire stages of education.

Chapter-2

REVIEW OF RELATED LITERATURE

A review of the research literature gives the investigator an idea of the kind of research work done so far on the field under study and assists the researcher to make the suitable research design and gather necessary tools as would be appropriate for the topic that the researcher has selected. The researcher comes to know the research gaps and issues pertaining to his or her field of investigation after going through the review of literature. The researcher can go through the scales of measurement utilized by the other researchers and see their reliability and validity and select the required tools appropriately according to his study. After analysing the research method of other researchers in the review of literature the researcher can get a broad frame regarding how to design his research and what suitable methodology to follow. The statistical techniques employed by the previous researchers helps the investigator to select efficient statistical methods for a study. The suggestions given by the earlier researchers provides essential know how to the investigator to include them in his study and plan his or her study accordingly. The educational implications provided by the previous workers gives useful understanding to the investigator to include them in his study and plan his or her study accordingly.

A review of literature obtains the data from various sources such as-

1. Research papers
2. Books
3. Previous works on the topic
4. Articles from different journals

The following points list the importance of doing a review of literature -

1. It helps in summarizing and synthesizing the works done previously.
2. Based on the previous researches the researcher can add a lot to his or her topic.
3. A good know how of existing works helps the researcher in his work.
4. A review of literature lends a direction to the current research.
5. It helps in summarizing into a brief account the previous works.
6. It restructures and reorganises the previous information.

7. It critically evaluates the older works.
8. The researcher gets familiarized with the previous works.
9. It assists in doing an appraisal of the previous works.
10. The worker identifies various sources of information.
11. Researcher can evaluate the previous works.
12. A correlation of previous works with the present study can be done.
13. Researcher can compare and contrast the older researches.
14. It gives an in depth understanding about the topic.
15. It sets the background for the research.
16. Lays down plan on how to examine the results.
17. Highlights the works that have been carried out on the topic already.
18. It gives information on the current state of the selected field of work.
19. It helps to identity the gaps in the researches done so far.
20. It helps to tell how the present work is different from previous researches.

The following points show the need for conducting a review of literature-

1. It helps to demonstrate how the present work can be fitted in a larger area of study.
2. The researcher is provided with an overview of the sources studied so far.
3. It interpretes available literature in view of recent developments in the area of study.
4. Progress of knowledge can be mapped and impact of information can be assessed.
5. Contradictions between different results can be known to the researcher.
6. Research gaps can be scrutinized and value can be added to the work.
7. Researcher can know how far is the work relevant.
8. It brings to light the topics that need further research.
9. It helps to form the research question.
10. The theoretical framework of the research can be set up.
11. An appropriate methodology for the investigation can be formed.
12. Obtained results can be compared with previous researches.
13. It helps to make the research more trustworthy.
14. Researcher can proceed in an original way for his or her work after literature review.
15. The rationale and the need for doing the study is provided by literature review.
16. Researcher can accurately collect data and follow methodology different from others.

17. Researcher can know what has already been done, accepted, or rejected on the topic.
18. The investigator can know the controversial areas of research.
19. The problems which are unsolved in the given field can be known.
20. The worker can be acquainted with emerging approaches and trends.

This present chapter presents a summary of the existing literature concerning the recent research problem. The literature review related to this problem is organized in chronological order starting from the latest. National and international studies found by the researcher, related to Vocational Interest, Study Habits and Socio-economic Status (SES) are given below:

2.1. Reviews related to Vocational Preferences

2.2. Reviews related to Study Habits

2.3. Review related to Socio-economic Status.

2.1. LITERATURE REVIEW ON VOCATIONAL INTEREST

Mondal, G. and Majumder, P. (2018) carried out a research on Vocational Interests of Secondary School Students in relation to their Gender. The purpose of the study was to determine the vocational interest of secondary level school students in relation to and their gender. A sample of 200 students (105 Boys and 95 Girls) reading in various schools in the district of Murshidabad of West Bengal state was selected by purposive sampling is method for the study. A standardised tool developed by Bansal V. P & Srivastava D. N. (1975) named as "Vocational Interest Record" were for collection of primary data. The data were analyzed with the help of Mean, SD and 't' test to study the vocational interests of secondary students. The result revealed that there existed difference in the vocational interest pattern of secondary school students in different vocational interest areas. The result also revealed that there is significant difference in the vocational areas of secondary school students in relation to gender is variation.

Hoque, J. (2018) did a study on vocational interests of secondary school Students in relation to their level of Aspiration. It is the simple reality that every people in the world have to choose any profession or work in their respective fields for sustaining their and livelihoods. If the chosen profession is of their own choice and interest, then they can excel in their field of work and the productivity will be greater. Now a days students and their family are more concern about their future. In this regard a study has been conducted to know the vocational interests in relation to level of aspiration. The main objectives of the study were, 1) To find the relationship between Vocational Interests and Level of Aspiration of the secondary school students. 2) To know the relationship among vocational interests and level of aspiration of the male secondary school students. 3) To find the relationship between vocational interests and level of aspiration of the female secondary school students. For this study a sample of 100 secondary school students (50 males and 50 females) have been selected. The tools employed for the research were 'Vocational Interest Scale' by Dr. Parveen Begum and 'Level of Aspiration Test (LOA)' developed by Dr. V.P. Bhargava. The data were analyzed with the help of Mean, Standard Deviation and correlation. The study revealed that there was no significant relationship between vocational interests and level of aspiration of the secondary level students. Another finding was that there was no significant relationship between vocational interests and level of aspiration of the male secondary school students. The researcher has not found any significant relationship between the vocational interests and level of aspiration of the female secondary school students. This study will be helpful for the teachers, parents, counsellor.

Mondal, G. C. (2018) conducted a Study of Vocational Interests of Secondary School Students in relation to their Parental Factors. The study investigated the influence of parent's occupation, monthly income and educational background on vocational interests of secondary school students. A sample of 200 students (105 Boys and 95 Girls) reading in different schools of the district of Murshidabad of West Bengal state was selected by purposive sampling method for the study. A standardised tool developed by Bansal V. P. & Srivastava D. N. (1975) named as "Vocational Interest Record" were employed for the collection of primary data. The data were analysed with the help of Mean, SD and percentage to study the vocational interests of secondary students influencing parental factors. The result revealed that there exists a strong difference in vocational interest pattern of secondary school students in terms of parental monthly and income. The result also revealed that there is a significant difference in the vocational area of secondary school students in relation to their parental educational background and occupation.

Bruce et al. (2017) led an investigation on Motivation for Occupational Preference among students of the regional maritime university in Nungua, Accra-Ghana. The cross-sectional survey design was picked up for the investigation. The stratified sampling method was utilized to choose a sample of 305 students from three departments forming a significant project of the study. The motivation for Occupational Preference Scale was utilized to assemble information from the object population. The Independent samples t-test and Analysis of Variance (ANOVA) were utilized to examine the information assembled. Results demonstrated that extrinsic or extraneous values impacted occupational stress more than instinctive values, both Ghanaian and International students were affected similarly by extrinsic or extraneous factors in their preference for occupation, there was no significant sexual orientation contrast in the impact of extrinsic or extraneous factors on occupational preference and there was a significant distinction in the intrinsic variables that impacted occupational preference among students from various programmes. It is in this way suggested customary vocation guidance and counseling sessions are held at different levels of education to illuminate and teach students particularly at the college on the advantages of profession preference dependent on natural variables than exclusively on outward factors. Taking everything into account, students must be urged to evaluate their professional intrigue or profession preference with the goal that they seek after projects and courses that they have a normal tendency for and not just settle on a decision of occupation or vocation only for outward qualities or prizes.

Bilos, A. et al. (2017) did investigation on Mobile Learning Usage and Preferences of Vocational Secondary School Students. The study concentrated on investigating students' cell phone utilization propensities, their frames of mind toward instruction or education with regards to versatile application support, and preferences in regards to portable learning highlights. The reliability and validity of the research tools and questionnaires was high. The discoveries give bits of knowledge into the conceivable outcomes of m-learning usage while making a structure for m-learning application improvement in the VET secondary school condition.

Juneja and Rikhi (2017) studied the Influence of Family Environment and Work Values on Vocational Preference across Career Stages in Young Adults. The present research went to concentrate on the role of the family environment and work values in deciding the professional preference and work values crosswise over vocation stages. The participants were individuals certainly enrolled in college, the individuals who had been working for under 2 years after post-graduation and those working for under 10 years, the sample estimate is 120. The measures utilized in the investigation were General Health Questionnaire-12, Family Environment Scale, Vocational Preference Inventory and Values Scale.The reliability and validity of the research tools and questionnaires was high. Regression analysis was utilized to examine the connection between the factors. The investigation has clinical implications for underlining the significance of settling on an increasingly arranged profession choice and assessing different angles in vocation stream ingenuity or change.

Kumar, R. (2017) attempted to find the vocational interests of secondary students. In this study, Vocational Interest Inventory developed by investigator himself was used. 100 students (50 male and 50 female) studying in the 10th class of Government Senior Secondary school of district Kangra in Himachal Pradesh were selected for the purpose of data collection in this study. The data was calculated with the help of Mean, S.D., and t-test to study the vocational interest of secondary students. The reliability and validity of the research tools and questionnaires was high.

Sk. R. R. (2017) conducted a study to ascertain the relationship between frustration and vocational preferences of senior secondary students. For this purpose a sample of 873 (436 male and 437female) senior secondary students, was randomly selected from schools of Aligarh district, U.P. Descriptive type of research design was used for the present study. In order to obtain the requisite information needed for the study Frustration test and Samvaidhna's Vocational Preference Scale (VPS) was employed by the investigator. In order to find out the relationship among variables viz. Frustration, and vocational preferences, the Product Moment Correlation, t-test, and ANOVA statistical techniques were used by the investigator. Results showed that no significant correlation was found between frustration and vocational preferences. The reliability and validity of the research tools and questionnaires was high. It was also found that the vocational interest of male students is higher than female counterparts. Moreover, government school students show higher vocational preference than private senior secondary students.

Choch, R. K. and Ajay, C. (2017) conducted a study on a Psychological Study of Vocational Interest among Secondary Students. In this study investigator used stratified random sample. The sample of the present study was 60, among them 30 Boys and 30 Girls is in 15 SSC and HSC students. They were selected and at random from various schools in Jetpur city, Gujarat. Tool Subject was administered Dr. J. H. Shan and Dr. Surekha Amin (1994) "Occupational Interest Inventory" (OII). The scale consists of 120 items and divided into 10 interest field by Kudar, here is the information about the test. The reliability and validity of the research tools and questionnaires was high. The test-retest reliability was found to be 0.74 and By Kuder Richardson method was found to be 0.86 both which was not only high but also statistically significant. Present research, information will be evaluated by scoring 'key' to get result. Following method will be used to explain the information. Kendall's Coefficient of Concordance method and was used. As per this classification, among the men, majority of them possessed science field interest and where as in the case of women, they have more interest in art vocational courses. However, the calculated 'W'- test value shows that there is significant relation between sex and vocational education interests. Hence, the hypothesis framed is unaccepted.

Sharma, D. K. (2016) conducted a study on influence school environment on vocational interest among adolescents. Careen has been defined as the total pattern of one's activities held during a person's life-time (Natalie, 2006). The career choice that adolescents make is a decision that is influenced not only by their development but also by the context in which they live (Chen, 1997). School environment is a powerful force and plays pivotal role in the all-round development, of the child. The reliability and validity of the research tools and questionnaires was high. Students in the developed world spend many hours in schools. School environment influences on vocational interest appeared to be a relatively new area of school influences on vocational interest appeared to be relatively new area of investigation. This research primarily focused on the role of teachers, classmates, peers influence or the interaction between teacher and children in vocational choice. The research showed that there is significant influence on vocational interest of school environment.

2.2. REVIEW RELATED TO STUDY HABITS:

Puju, J. A. and Khan, M.A. (2019) conducted on Self-concept and study habits of visually impaired and hearing impaired college going students. The present investigation has been carried out by following the objectives to study the self-concept and study habits of visually impaired and hearing impaired college going students. The investigators have selected 200 specially-abled students (100 visually impaired and other 100 hearing impaired) students from various govt. degree colleges in Kashmir province. The data was collected by using Sagar sharma self-concept inventory and Palsane Sharma Study habits inventory by following purposive sampling. The collected data was analyzed by using some statistical techniques. Some of the major findings have been drawn from the present study that there is significant difference between visually impaired and orthopedically challenged college going students on their self-concept and study habits.

Upadhyay (2017) carried out a study on the relationship of academic achievement among senior secondary students in relation to study habits. Investigator suggested that academic achievement was treated as dependent variable whereas study habit was treated as an independent variable. 300 senior secondary school students of New Delhi participated in the study using Stratified random sampling technique, and descriptive survey method was employed to gather the data. Study Habits Inventory by Mukhopadhyay and Sansanwal (2011) was used to examine the study habits among students and score of the class tenth was taken as a measure of academic achievement. The findings of the study revealed that no significant difference was found in the academic achievement of male and female senior secondary school students. Further, no significant difference was also found in the study habits of male and female senior secondary school students. The study was very meaningful . It was also reported that there exists a significant relationship between academic achievement and study habits of senior secondary school students.

K. Kaur (2017) conducted a study to examine the study habits of adolescents in relation to gender and locale. The study was intended to find the difference between mean scores of Study Habits of adolescents of Ludhiana. Two objectives were framed by the investigator, first, to study the significant difference in the mean scores of Study Habits of urban and rural male adolescents, second, to study the significant difference in the mean scores of Study Habits of male and female adolescents. A sample of 200 students was taken consisting of 100 male and 100 female students which further categorized into 100 rural and 100 urban adolescents of Ludhiana. Study Habit Inventory by Sri. Mukhopadhyay M (2002) was used to collect the data. The reliability and validity of the research tools and questionnaires was high. The study was very meaningful. The results of the study showed that there was significant difference exist between Study Habits of male and female adolescents of the rural and urban area of Ludhiana.

Singh, A. B. & Ahmad (2017) led a study to study the attitude of senior secondary school students towards Continuous and Comprehensive Evaluation (CCE) on their study habits in Allahabad. Attitude towards CCE was measured by CCE Attitude Scale developed by investigator and Study Habits of the students towards CCE was assessed by the Study Habit Inventory constructed by Dr. M. Mukhopadhyay and Dr. D.N. Sansanwal. The reliability and validity of the research tools and questionnaires was high. The study was very meaningful. A sample of 200 students of the senior secondary school of CBSE board of Allahabad has been taken for the study through simple random technique. The study showed that there was a significant positive correlation between the attitude of senior secondary school students towards CCE and their study habits and students had fairly favourable study habits exhibited fairly favourable attitude towards CCE. Further, investigators concluded that there exists a significant difference between most favourable and least favourable group of attitude towards Continuous and Comprehensive Evaluation of students on their study habits and Attitude of male and female students do not differ significantly towards CCE.

2.3 REVIEW RELATED TO SOCIO-ECONOMIC STATUS (SES)

Ali, M.R & Sk, R.R. (2019) conducted a study on achievement motivation and socio-economic status among senior secondary students in Aligarh district. A sample of 200 (100 male and 100 female) senior secondary students was selected. For analysis and interpretation of data correlation, regression analysis and "t" test used by the researcher. The investigator found that there is a significant relationship between achievement motivation and SES. Also SES shows significant positive effect on Achievement motivation.

In addition, study participants tended to agree that mobile learning will play a significant role in education in the future. The paper also explored the reported differences among the students in the three countries and suggested several implications for understanding students' views of mobile learning. The findings provide insights into possibilities of m-learning implementation while creating a framework for m-learning application development in the VET secondary school environment.

Bruce et al. (2017) found out motivation for occupational preference among Regional Maritime University students. The cross-sectional survey design was chosen for the study and the stratified sampling technique was used to select a sample of 305 students from three departments constituting major programmes of study. Motivation for Occupational Preference Scale was used to gather data from the sampled population. The researcher utilized the required scales and questionnaire for the study which had a high level of coefficient of correlation of reliability and validity. The Independent samples t-test and Analysis of Variance (ANOVA) were used to analyze the data gathered. Results showed that, extrinsic values influenced occupational preference more than intrinsic values, both Ghanaian and International students were influenced equally by extrinsic factors in their preference for occupation, there was no significant gender difference in the influence of extrinsic factors on occupational preference and there was a significant difference in the intrinsic factors that influence occupational preference among students from different and programmes. It is therefore recommended that, regular career guidance and counselling sessions are held at various levels of education to inform and educate students especially at the university on the benefits of career preference based on intrinsic factors than solely on extrinsic factors. In conclusion students must be encouraged to assess their vocational interest or career preference so that they pursue programmes and courses that they have the natural inclination for and not only make a choice of vocation or career just for extrinsic values or rewards.

Nadeem N.A. and Ahmad I (2016) investigated the career preferences of male and female higher secondary students. The study was conducted on a sample of 200 higher secondary students (N= 100 males & 100 females) studying in 12th class in various government Higher secondary institutes of district Budgam. The sample was drawn on random basis. Bhargava and Bhargava's career preference record were used to collect data from the selected sample. Percentage statistics were used to analyses the data is collected. The researcher utilized the required scales and questionnaire for the study which had a high level of coefficient of correlation of reliability and validity. The study was very meaningful. The study revealed that the male and female higher secondary students differ with respect to their career preference.

Fouad, N.A. et.al. (2016) examined the nomological network for the Family Influence Scale in the United States and India. Specifically, the study assessed the relationship between family influences on career decision making and the constructs of family obligation, work volition, calling, work values, and occupational engagement across two countries. The researcher utilized the required scales and questionnaire for the study which had a high level of coefficient of correlation of reliability and validity. A total of 136 U.S. participants and 377 participants from India responded to a survey via Amazon Mechanical Turk. The study found support for the construct validity and the four different types of family influences both between the United States and the Indian population. Family influence was correlated in expected ways with family obligation, The purpose of this study was to investigate the effects of parental influence and on adolescents' career choice on secondary schools students in Badagry Local Government Area of Lagos State.The research was very purposeful. The sample consisted of three hundred respondents who were randomly selected from ten purposely selected secondary schools (3 Model Colleges, 4 Non-Model Colleges, and 3 Private Colleges). The instrument used was a questionnaire which was administered to the respondents personally by the researcher. Five (5) null hypotheses were formulated and tested. Chi-square, using analysis of contingency table was used to test the hypotheses. All hypotheses were tested at the 0.05 level of significance of variable of sex, class of school, and type of school as to the effects of parental influence on adolescents' career choice on secondary schools students in the Local Government Area. The findings of the study showed that 48.36% of the respondents agreed to parents influencing their career choice. On the average, 21.5% of the respondents agreed that their parents' line of business influenced their career choice, while 78.5% disagreed. On the whole, 30% of the respondents agreed that they chose the family career because is they need to sustain the family business. In addition, three (3) out of the five (5) null hypotheses tested were accepted because there were no significant differences in the variables compared. These were hypotheses 1, 3, and 5. Hypotheses 2 and 4 were rejected as there were significant differences in the variables compared. The results of these findings seem to indicate that adolescents in secondary schools in Badagry Local Government Area of Lagos State have some form of independence in making career choices.

Eremie, M.D. (2015) studied the variables affecting career choices among Senior Secondary School Students in Rivers State, Nigeria. Simple random sampling techniques were adopted to select four hundred (400) Senior Secondary School Student from five Secondary Schools in Rivers State. The "Comprehensive Career Choice Survey" (CCCS) was administered to the respondents to collect necessary data. The t-test statistics and was used to test three null hypotheses at 0.05 level of significance. The researcher utilized the required scales and questionnaire for the study which had a high level of coefficient of correlation of reliability and validity. The research was very purposeful. The findings revealed that there were significant differences among male and female secondary school students in their career choices in terms of: Prestige of a profession, gender parity, and parental influence. Based on the findings some recommendations were made: (1) Professional career counsellors should be consulted to assist students in planning and choosing their careers. (2) Professional career counsellors should include the students in the selecting process, considering interest, ability, skills and personality of the students.

Mattoo, M.I. (2013) carried out a study to find the career choices of students at secondary level. A sample of 200 students was drawn randomly from 12 secondary schools of district Srinagar within the age range of 16 plus. The selected sample is comprised of arts and science streams. Chatterji's Non-Language Preference Record was administered to collect the data. The research was very purposeful. The researcher utilized the required scales and questionnaire for the study which had a high level of coefficient of correlation of reliability and validity. Also, parental education as one of the variables was also taken into consideration. Data was subjected to statistical treatment by applying percentages and 't' values. The results revealed some significant differences on the basis of gender and parental education in various career choices of the subjects under investigation.

Monika et.al (2014) conducted an investigation on a total of 50 students of Department of Physical Education of CDLU Sirsa. The subjects were in the age group of 20-25 years. Out of total sample of 50 players, 25 were male and 25 were female. The Vocational interest record constructed and standardised by V.P. Bansal was used for collecting the data. The research was very purposeful. The purpose of the study was to find the difference between the vocational interests of boy and girl students of department of Physical Education of Chaudhary Devi Lal University, Sirsa. The researcher used the t test for analyzing the data. In the present study it has been found that the students of department of Physical Education differ significantly in inter-vocational interests. The researcher utilized the required scales and questionnaire for the study which had a high level of coefficient of correlation of reliability and validity. The research was very purposeful. These findings show that with the spread of educational opportunities and the explosion of knowledge almost all the students are aware of the present development in the field of physical education. And this awareness has helped then in bringing the gap among various students with regard to the vocational choices. The female students have poor vocational interests; the cause might be such that the female students are not equally exposed to the educational opportunities like male again.

2.4. RESEARCH GAPS AND ISSUES:

After making a critical and careful appraisal of all the previously conducted research studies the researcher has observed the research gaps that there is no research done on the present problem. The studies are conducted either on one variable or by taking two variables which are in the present research. It is also found from the above literature that all the studies have been done on the vocational interests, study habits and SES among normal students. There were very few studies on the concerned variables between visually challenged adolescents. Some works focused on various streams of pupils, such as science, commerce, university students and different kinds of institutes.Researches have also been conducted on higher education. Few research works are related to students at the undergraduate level. Some research works are focused on finding the effect and relation of one independent variable with other dependent variable or variables. It is observed that very few researches are carried out which are in a direct way aimed on comparing the regular and distance modes of students at the undergraduate level specifically including the variables like vocational interests, socio economic status, and demographic variables. Few studies relate to only vocational interests, others study only socio economic status, or only the demographic factors. Some studies are relevant to regular education while others are relevant for distance or non-formal mode of education separately. In a very small number of research works, one variable is seen in relation to other variable or more variables.

Some researches that conducted among visually impaired students which are:

Dale and Salt (2017) described the development of a "Early Support Developmental Journal" for use with young visually impaired children and babies that provides a structured sequential guide of expected The researcher utilized the required scales and questionnaire for the study which had a high level of coefficient of correlation of reliability and validity. developmental steps in young children with visual impairment aged 0–36 months. Builds on the current research and knowledge of the Developmental Vision team and other researchers and practitioners and expands on the guide providing more finely graded steps of key developmental sequences especially and in the areas of object relationships and reasoning, communication and social development, language and meaning, play and learning, movement and mobility and self-help skills.

Douglas et al. (2015) tested the reading ability of 476 children with low vision, using an unmodified print version of the Neale Analysis of Reading Ability (NARA). The data showed that the average reading ages for accuracy, comprehension and speed for the sample are generally below their chronological age when the comparison is made with their fully sighted peers.

Greaney et al. (1998) checked the reading of 317 Braille readers (in the UK and Ireland) using a Braille version of the NARA. As in the study with low vision, the data showed that the average reading ages for accuracy, comprehension and speed for the sample are generally below their chronological age when the comparison is made with their fully sighted peers (and low-vision readers). Again, the size of the "lag" increases with age. In the case of Braille, however, there appeared to be a greater lag in reading speed.

Hull and Mason (1993, 1995) made a specialised tactile version of a test for speed of information-processing, working with 318 children in the UK and Ireland. A significant finding was that the speed of access of the blind children was considerably less than that of sighted children using print versions of the similar test (two to three times slower, depending on the format)

O'Connell et al. (2006) spoke about tactile modelling and physical guidance as teaching strategies are explored and described in detail and conclude that they are effective methods of improving the motor skills and physical activities of students who are blind. They highlighted that it is imperative and that the issues of personal space, fear of liability and lack of one-to-one instruction should be anticipated and overcome.

Lieberman (2002) surveyed physical education teachers about the barriers to including children with visual impairment in lessons; professional preparation was identified as the dominant barrier.

Hill et al. (2005) observed delays in speed, accuracy and comprehension of print reading among British children with low vision. They made a distinction between developmental delays in reading and difficulties in access to text, arguing that long-term difficulty in accessing text leads to developmental delays.

Gompel et al. 2004) found that, despite their lower reading speed on a reading-comprehension task, the children with low vision comprehended texts at least as well as sighted children.

So after carrying out a review of the research gaps the investigator has decided to choose the present topic. Thus the researcher aims to carry out a study of vocational interest among visually challenged adolescents in relation to certain personal, familial and demographic variables.

Chapter-3

RESEARCH METHODOLOGY AND DESIGN

The present chapter deals with the methodology and design followed by the researcher. This is the most prominent proportion of research. Because the significance, relevance and researchability of the problem selected by a researcher for investigation, the methodology followed is also significant for determining usefulness and generalizability of the findings. Sometime, the problem has been properly defined and the tools have been carefully chosen, but inadequate methodology followed may mislead results. The earlier two chapters are the comprehensive discussion of the theoretical background and review of related literature. The present chapter dedicated to the methodology followed in conducting this research i.e. description of variables, population and sampling, tools, statistical technique etc.

Present chapter deals with design and methodology adopted in this study. An attempt has been made to study the relationship of frustration with Vocational Interest, Study Habits and Socio-economic Status (SES) among Visually Challenged adolescents. In these concerns, the methodology has been presented in the following:

3. Methodology and Design

3.1 Description of the Variables under study

3.2 Population and Sample

3.3 Research Tools are used

3.4 Collection of Data

3.5 Statistical Techniques used

3. METHODOLOGY AND DESIGN

Methodology and design tell the researcher- what and how to do the work accurately. It has been determined from time to time that a suitable research design guards against the collection of irrelevant data. It also helps the researcher in formulating and testing the hypotheses by reaching valid and objective conclusion regarding the relationship between independent and dependent variables. The selection of any research design is obviously not based on the whims of the researcher, rather it is based on the purpose of the investigation, types of variables and conditions in which the research is conducted.

In the present chapter the methodology details of this work are dealt with. By and large, the methodology followed in this study has been worked out in accordance with its objectives. The present research work uses descriptive type of research design. Descriptive research deals with the relationships between variables, testing hypotheses, and development of principles or theories that have universal validity for generalization. It is correlational in nature as the correlation between dependent and independent variables have been discovered and predictions are made. The purpose of the study is to determine the level and effect of Study Habit and Socio-economic Status (SES) among Visually Challenged Adolescents and their relationship with vocational Interest.

3.1. Description of the Variables Under Study:

The contemporary research work aims at examining the Vocational Interest among Visually Challenged adolescents in relation to their Study Habit and Socio-economic Status (SES). In this study Vocational Interest is taken as Dependent Variable while Study Habit and Socio-economic Status (SES) are taken as Independent Variables. An independent variable is changed or controlled in a scientific experiment to test the effects on the dependent variables whereas a dependent variable is tested and measured in a scientific experiment. The dependent variable is 'dependent' on the independent variable. While changing the independent variables, the effect on the dependent variable is observed and recorded. In this study attempt to find out the relationship, effect and mean difference between Independent and Dependent Variables among Visually Challenged adolescents.

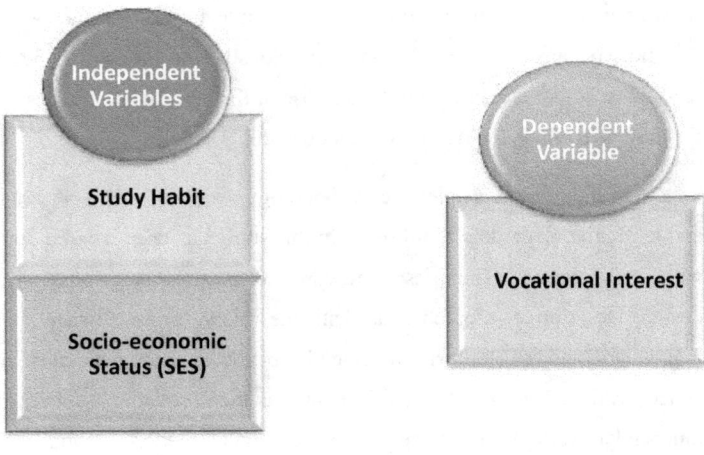

Figure 3.1: Description of Variables under Study

3.2 POPULATION AND SAMPLE:

A population is any group of individuals that have one or more characteristics in common and that is of interest of the researcher (Best and Kahn, 2012). It may be all the individuals of a particular type or a restricted part of that group (Best, 1977). A population is also called a universe by some statisticians (Koul, 1984). Therefore, a population denotes to any collection of a specified group of human beings or of non-human units. The population, in statistical investigations, is always arbitrarily defined (Guilford and Fruchter, 1978) by naming its unique properties. However, in social science describes the term "Population" in a comprehensive sense to include all sets of individuals, objects or reactions having a unique combination of qualities. The statistical indices computed using the entire population (if possible) is called "parameters". The present study is grounded on a population of Visually Challenged Adolescents of Uttar Pradesh and Uttarakhand. Thus, all those adolescents challenged with visual impairment constituted the population of the study.

Sample:

A sample is a small proportion of the population that is selected for observation and analysis (Best and Kahn, 2012). It helps to reduce expenditure, save time and energy, permits measurement of greater scope, or produce greater precision and accuracy (Koul, 1984). A measure based on samples is termed as "statistics". "In social science, on many occasions, the population is imaginative. Opposing to population samples are not selected haphazardly. They are selected in a systematic random way, and the operation of probability is utilized. Where random selection is not possible, other systematic means are used (SK, 2019)." In this study, convenient sampling method has been used in the choice of schools situated in districts of Aligarh and Dehradun situated in Western U.P and of Uttarakhand respectively. In this research, the sample consisted of 200 Visually Challenged Adolescents selected from Ahmadi School for Blind and National Institute for the Visually Handicapped (VIVH). Out of these 200 students, 100 selected from Ahmadi School for Blind and 100 selected from National Institute for the Visually Handicapped (NIVH).

The table 3.1 makes available details of the Sample.

Table 3.1
Details of the Sample

S. No	School Name	Sample		Total
		Male	Female	
1	Ahmadi School for Blind, Aligarh	50	50	100
2	National Institute for the Visually Handicapped (NIVH)	50	50	100

Table 3.2
Showing the Distribution of Data

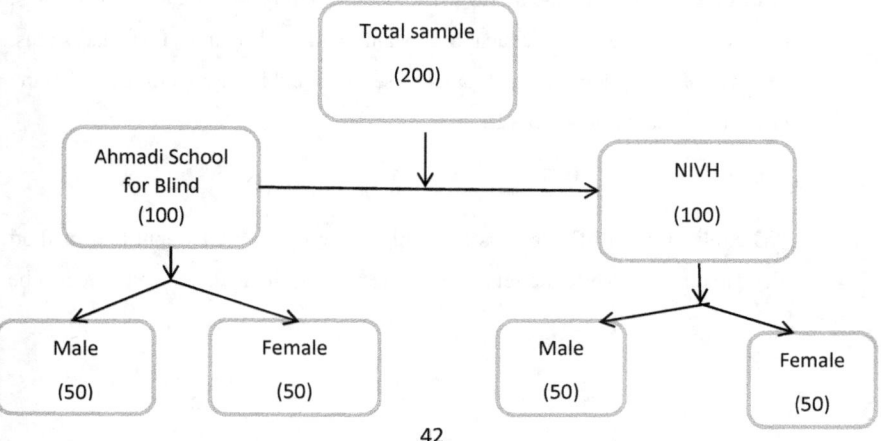

3.3 RESEARCH TOOLS USED:

In order to obtain the essential information for the study, following research tools are employed: (i) Samvaidhna's Vocational Preference Scale (VPS) (ii) Socio-economic Status Scale (iii) Test of Study Habits and Attitudes (TSHA). The details about these tools are described below:

3.3.1 Vocational Preference Scale (VPS):

To ascertain Vocational Interest among Visually Challenged adolescents the investigator used Samvaidhna's Vocational Preference Scale (VPS) developed by Dr. Amit Abraham and Dr. Rashmi Pant. This test was published by Agra Psychological Research Cell (2004). This scale has been developed on the basis of literature available (Cherry 1974, Gianakos Irene 1999, Laurie 1995, Mohan and Vohra 1981, Upreti and Upreti 1984) and a research study done by the authors (2002) entitled "A study of values of undergraduate and postgraduate students as determinants of their vocational preferences." This scale originally consisted of 156 positively worded vocation-based statements. Finally, for the balancing ten statements each for each of the nine vocations was selected amounting to a total of 90 statements.

3.3.2. The Socio Economic Status Scale

To measure the Socio-economic condition of the Visually Challenged adolescents the Socio-economic Status Scale (SESS) was employed. This is a latest tool which is developed by Dr. Ashok K. Kalia and Dr. Sudhir Sahu in 2012. Socio-economic Status of an individual in this scale means "Status of his or her family in relation to their level of sociocultural participation, ability to influence the masses, kind of occupation, level of education, health and well-being, financial status, lifestyle, level of aspiration, kinds of gadgets, services and leisure facilities which the family has" (Kalia and Sudhir, 2012).

Reliability

The reliability of SES scale is fairly high. The reliability by split half method was calculated at 0.68 while the reliability by test-retest method was computed to be 0.86.

Validity

The scale has fairly high face validity as the items were developed after careful discussions with eminent scholars and survey of literature and tests on socio economic status. The content validity was assured adequately as those items have been selected only which had hundred percent agreements with the judges as regards their relevance. The empirical validity of the SES scale is also fairly high as it has been used by many researchers and students. A criterion validity value of 0.85 was calculated for this scale after correlating it with the socio economic status scale of Dr. Rajbir Singh, Dr. S. Kumar, and Dr. Radhey Shyam (2006).

Scoring

The scoring of SES scale is very simple. In order to calculate the complete score of a respondent in this scale, the examiner has to sum up the scores of the boxes where the respondent has put a tick mark according to the scoring key developed for the SES scale.

3.3.3 Test of Study Habits and Attitudes (TSHA)

For assessing the Study Habits of the Visually Challenged adolescents, the Test of Study Habits and Attitudes was used in the present study which is a standardized and developed by Dr. C.P. Mathur (2002) and has been published by National Psychological Corporation, Agra. This test measures the Study Habits of the students. First, the respondents filled up personal data at the blanks printed on the front page. The investigator read out the instructions clearly and loudly printed on the front page of the consumable booklet and make sure that students have understood the mode of recording their responses. The test is suitable for use with both the sexes.

This test is constructed on nine major areas of the study techniques, habits and attitudes, viz.,

1. Attitude towards Teachers;
2. Home Environment;
3. Attitude towards Education;
4. Study Habits;
5. Mental Conflict;
6. Concentration;

7. Home Assignment;
8. Self-Conflict;
9. Examination.

It encloses 60 items. A high score on this test indicates the high order of correct study habits and proper attitudes, while a low score shows poor study techniques. It seeks to discriminate between good and poor study techniques of students, and is expected to be helpful to teachers and counsellors to know their students' techniques of study in a scientific way. A copy of TSHA has been attached in the appendix.

Scoring of TSHA:

A set of two scoring keys is provided for scoring the responses. Scoring key 'A' is meant to score the correct study habits and scoring key 'B' to know the items and corresponding areas in which the students need guidance. For the scoring purpose, take the scoring key and place it on the answer sheet. The two 'anchoring' points, one above and one below the column will be found helpful in setting the key accurately. Now count the number of correctly responded items visible through the perforations. This Number as per the key 'A' is the obtained score for correct study habits. Before starting to score, see that to how many items the testee has put √ in the column (?) count these and if the √ in the column (?) are more than 3, then categorize the testee according to the following norms:

00 to 03 ------------ Avoid considering

04 to 07 -------------Indecisive

07 to 12 -------------Confused and Indecisive

13 and more --------Highly confused and indecisive

Reliability of TSHA:

The reliability of this test was established by the test-retest method. Table 3.3 shows the reliability of the TSHA

Table 3.3
Reliability of TSHA

S. No.	Age	Reliability Coefficient	N
1	13 to 16	+0.87	200
2	16 and above	+0.89	200

Validity of TSHA:

For the determination of validity, the test has been validated with two tests of Study Habits as well as with Achievement (academic) scores on a representative sample of 200 students. The coefficients were found as shown in Table 3.4.

Table 3.4
Validity of TSHA

S. No.	N	Tests	r
1	200	Survey of Study Habits & Attitudes by C.P. Mathur	+0.63
2	200	Survey of Study Habits & Attitudes (General) by A. R. Purohit	+0.77
3	200	Academic Achievement Scores	+0.65

Administration:

The test contains 60 items seeking a response in 'Yes', 'Doubtful' and 'No'. Responses are obtained on a separate answer sheet and the test booklet can be used over and again. The test is non-time. Generally, 40 minutes have been found sufficient to deliver necessary instructions and obtain the responses.

Levels of Study Habits:

The study habits of the students were calculated through the scoring key described in previous section. The levels of study habits used in the research are as follows:

1. Poor Study Habits:	Scores lie below Mean -1 s.d.
2. Satisfactory Study Habits:	Scores lie between -1 s.d. to +1 s.d.
3. Good Study Habits:	Scores lie above Mean +1 s.d.

3.4 COLLECTION OF DATA:

The task of data collection was performed by the investigator himself. The investigator requested the principals or heads of the institutions to grant consent to collect data from Visually Challenged adolescents. After getting the permission, the investigator contacted the students and administered them the two tools during the same setting. Throughout the process of data collection, the investigator guaranteed the students that the information given in the sheets by them were for the purpose of research work only and would be kept confidential. This initiate along with the importance of this research work was highly trustworthy and provided in obtaining relevant and genuine data. The investigator administered two tools, Vocational Preference Scale (VPS) and Study Habit Scale to the students having Visual Impairment one by one with the help of Normal Collogue. The main purpose of the test is undoubtedly explained to the respondents. They are requested to listen the instruction carefully and clear doubts. No item should be omitted and there is nothing 'right' or 'wrong' about the statements. There is no time limit; however, half an hour was sufficient for their response.

3.5 STATISTICAL TECHNIQUES USED:

The statistical techniques used in the present work are-

(i) Correlation Coefficient

(ii) 't' test.

(iii) Regression Analysis

Chapter-4

DATA ANALYSIS, INTERPRETATION & DISCUSSION OF RESULT

The present chapter includes data analysis, interpretation and discussion of results. Analysis and interpretation of collected data is considered as the sole task of any research work that demands ample energy and patience from the investigator. Further, the adequacy and trustworthiness of research tools, the dependability of research findings have a strong relationship with the statistical techniques used in data analysis. Statistics are considered fundamental to research work. Without employing it no research work impossible to conduct. Mainly statistics consent thorough description of information and power us to be confident in our thinking and other procedures of analysis.

Analysis and interpretation are the systematic process of allocating statistical method to the collection of information and determination of conclusions, significance, and implication of the findings (Sk, 2019). The task analysis and interpretation initiate with the purpose of transformation of obtained data into credible evidence about the development of the interference and its performance (Sk, 2019). Therefore, in any research analysis explains the results given by the acquired data and interpretation discloses the meaning of results following the objectives of the study. Hence, to obtain the desired outcomes and their scientific explanation, it is essential to confirm that the data should be well organized to facilitate the present study carried out by the investigator.

In this study, the obtained data analysed and intereepreted by the investigator using the appropriate statistical technique to make sure about the relationship between independent variables (Study Habit and Socio-economic Status) and the dependent variable (Vocational Interest). Researcher also try to make the comparison among variables with respect to their gender and locality. In the present study the investigator, fit the raw score in MS Excel (2013) and later, pass on the raw score into IBMSPSS-20.0 software (IBM Statistical Package for Social Science) for analysis of data. The current chapter contains the analysis and interpretation of data which done by the investigator are given below:

4.1   Study of Correlation

4.2   Study of Regression Analysis

4.3   Study of Mean Differences

4.1 STUDY OF CORRELATION:

Correlation is the relationship between two or more paired variables or two or more sets of data. The degree of relationship measured and represented by the coefficient of correlation. This coefficient may be identified by either the letter "r", the Greek Letter "rho", or other symbols, depending on the data distributions and the way the coefficient has been calculated. This type of relationship is defined into three way positive, negative and zero correlation. When two variables associate in that way that as one increase, the other tend to increase called positive correlation. Sometimes variables are negatively correlated when a large amount of one variable is associated with a small amount of the other. As one increase, the other tend to decrease. When the relationship between two sets of variables is a pure chance relationship, we say that there is no correlation or zero correlation. The degree of linear correlation can be represented quantitatively by the coefficient of correlation. A perfect positive correlation is +1.00. A perfect negative correlation is -1.00. A complete lack of correlation is zero (0).

In social science, while the researcher calculated correlation 0.01 & 0.05 level of significance are accepted. The researcher, in this study, used 0.01 & and 0.05 level of significance while inferring the results. In this study researcher calculated coefficient of correlation between Independent Variables (Study habit, Socio-economic Status) and Dependent Variable (Vocational Interest). The calculated values are given below along with objectives 1 to 2.

Objective:

1. To ascertain the significance relationship between Vocational Interest and Study habits (Personal Variable) among Visually challenged adolescents.

1.1. To ascertain the significance relationship between High Vocational Interest and High-Level Study habits (Personal Variable) among Visually challenged adolescents.

1.2. To ascertain the significance relationship between Low Vocational Interest and Low-Level Study habits (Personal Variable) among Visually challenged adolescents.

2. To ascertain the significance relationship between Vocational Interest and Socio-economic Status (Familial Variable) among Visually challenged adolescents.

2.1. To ascertain the significance relationship between High Vocational Interest and High-level Socio-economic Status (Familial Variable) among Visually challenged adolescents.

2.2. To ascertain the significance relationship between Low Vocational Interest and Low-level Socio-economic Status (Familial Variable) among Visually challenged adolescents.

4.1.1 Correlation Matrix for the Combined Sample:

Table-4.1 represent the intercorrelation among the three variables (Vocational Interest, Study Habit and Socio-economic Status) for the sample of 200 visually challenged adolescents. The study of correlation table 4.1 gives estimating results. All the coefficient of correlation was significant at 0.01 level. The Vocational Interest correlates significantly with Study Habit and Socio-economic status at 0.01 level.

Table-4.1
Correlation Matrix for Combined Variables

Variables	Vocational Interest	Study Habit	Socio-economic Status
Vocational Interest	1	.886**	.968**
Study Habit		1	956**
Socio-economic Status			1

**Significant at 0.01 level of confidence (2 tailed)

Objective 1: To ascertain the significance relationship between Vocational Interest and Study Habits (Personal Variable) among Visually challenged adolescents.

The first objective of this study was to know the relationship between Vocational Interest and Study Habits (Personal Variable) of Visually Challenged Adolescents. So as to achieve this objective, the investigator frames the following null hypothesis for empirical verification

Hypothesis (Ho$_1$): There is no significant relationship between Vocational Interest and Study Habits (Personal Variable) among Visually Challenged adolescents.

With the aim of find out the relationship between Vocational Interest and Study Habits (Personal Variable) among Visually Challenged adolescents, the investigator first calculates the scores of the participant by using Pearson Product Moment Coefficient of Correlation for the total sample. The table-4.2 represents Number of Sample, Degree of Freedom of the Sample and Value of the Pearson Product Moment Coefficient of Correlation along with its Significant Value (P-Value).

Table 4.2
Showing the relationship between Vocational Interest and Study Habits (Personal Variable) among Visually Challenged Adolescents.

Variables	N	Df	Calculated "r"	p- Value
Vocational Interest	200	198	.886**	.000
Study Habits				

**Significant at 0.01 level of confidence (2 tailed)

The table 4.2 illustrates the intercorrelation between Vocational Interest and Study Habit (Personal Variable) among Visually Challenged Adolescents for the total sample 200. The calculated values on the table 4.2 reveals that there is a positive and significant relationship between Vocational interest and Study habits. The Calculated Coefficient of Correlation (r- value) value for the total sample is .886 (P = .000) which is significant at 0.01 level of confidence. That means both variables

(Vocational Interest & Study Habit) are positively correlated which indicated the changed in values of one variable positively affect the other one. Therefore, the first null hypothesis **"There is no significant relationship between Vocational Interest and Study Habits (Personal Variable) among Visually Challenged adolescents"** is rejected.

Figure-4.1

Showing the Correlation between Vocational Interest and Study habit among Visually Challenged Adolescents

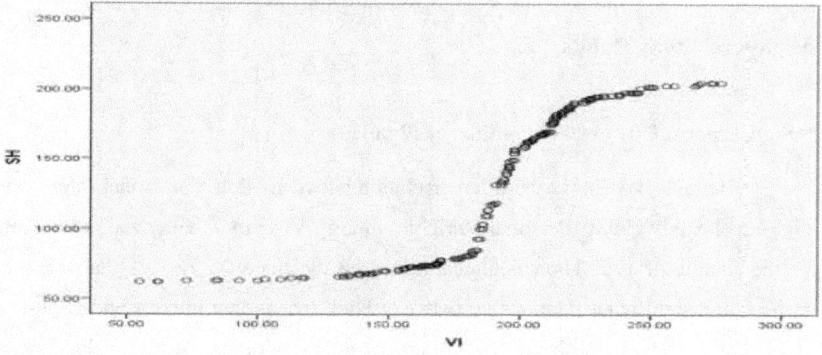

Objective 1.1: To ascertain the significance relationship between High Vocational Interest and High-Level Study habits (Personal Variable) among Visually challenged adolescents.

The first sub-objective of this study was to identify the relationship between High Vocational Interest and High-Level Study Habits (Personal Variable) of Visually Challenged Adolescents. Thus, to achieve this objective, the investigator formulates the following null hypothesis for experiential verification

Hypothesis (Ho$_{1.1}$): There is no significant relationship between High Vocational Interest and High-Level Study Habits (Personal Variable) among Visually Challenged adolescents.

In order to find out the relationship between High Vocational Interest and High-Level Study Habits (Personal Variable) among Visually Challenged adolescents, the investigator first calculates the scores of the participant by using Pearson Product Moment Coefficient of Correlation. The table-4.3 represents Number of Sample, Degree of Freedom of the Sample and Value of the Pearson Product Moment Coefficient of Correlation along with its Significant Value (P- Value).

Table 4.3

Showing the relationship between High Vocational Interest and High-level Study Habits (Personal Variable) among Visually Challenged Adolescents.

Variables	N	Df	Calculated "r"	p- Value
High Vocational Interest				
High-level Study Habits	100	98	.891**	.000

**Significant at 0.01 level of confidence (2 tailed)

The table 4.3 shows the intercorrelation between High Vocational Interest and High-level Study Habit (Personal Variable) among Visually Challenged Adolescents for the sample of 100. The calculated values on the table 4.2 reveals that there is a positive and significant relationship between High Vocational interest and High-level Study habits. The Calculated Coefficient of Correlation (r- value) value for the selected sample is .891 (P = .000) which is significant at 0.01 level of confidence. That means both variables (High Vocational Interest & High-level Study Habit) are positively correlated which indicated the changed in values of one variable positively affect the other one. Therefore, the first sub-null hypothesis **"There is no significant relationship between High Vocational Interest and High-level Study Habits (Personal Variable) among Visually Challenged adolescents"** is rejected.

Figure-4.2

Showing the Correlation between High Vocational Interest and High-level Study habit among Visually Challenged Adolescents

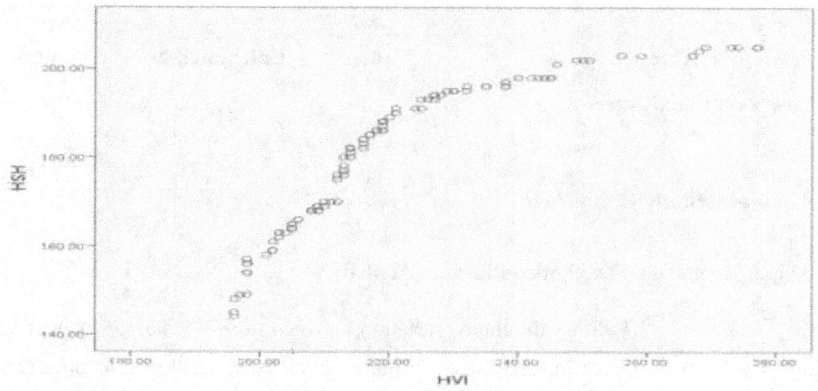

Objective 1.2: To ascertain the significance relationship between Low Vocational Interest and Low-Level Study habits (Personal Variable) among Visually challenged adolescents.

This objective of the study was to recognize the relationship between Low Vocational Interest and Low-Level Study Habits (Personal Variable) of Visually Challenged Adolescents. Thus, to accomplish this objective, the investigator formulates the following null hypothesis for empirical verification

Hypothesis (Ho$_{1.2}$): There is no significant relationship between Low Vocational Interest and Low-Level Study Habits (Personal Variable) among Visually Challenged adolescents.

In order to find out the relationship between Low Vocational Interest and Low-Level Study Habits (Personal Variable) among Visually Challenged adolescents, the investigator first calculates the scores of the participant by using Pearson Product Moment Coefficient of Correlation. The table-4.4 represents Number of Sample, Degree of Freedom of the Sample and Value of the Pearson Product Moment Coefficient of Correlation along with its Significant Value (P- Value).

Table 4.4
Showing the relationship between Low Vocational Interest and Low-level Study Habits (Personal Variable) among Visually Challenged Adolescents.

Variables	N	df	Calculated "r"	p- Value
Low Vocational Interest	100	98	.696**	.000
Low-level Study Habits				

**Significant at 0.01 level of confidence (2 tailed)

The table 4.4 shows the intercorrelation between Low Vocational Interest and Low-level Study Habit (Personal Variable) among Visually Challenged Adolescents for the sample of 100. The calculated values on the table 4.4 reveals that there is a positive and significant relationship between Low Vocational interest and Low-level Study habits. The Calculated Coefficient of Correlation (r- value) value for the selected sample is .696 (P = .000) which is significant at 0.01 level of confidence. That means both variables (Low Vocational Interest & Low-level Study Habit) are positively correlated which indicate that the changed in values of one variable positively affect the other one. Therefore, the null hypothesis **"There is no significant relationship between Low Vocational Interest and Low-level Study Habits (Personal Variable) among Visually Challenged adolescents"** is rejected.

Figure-4.3

Showing the Correlation between Low Vocational Interest and Low-level Study habit among Visually Challenged Adolescents

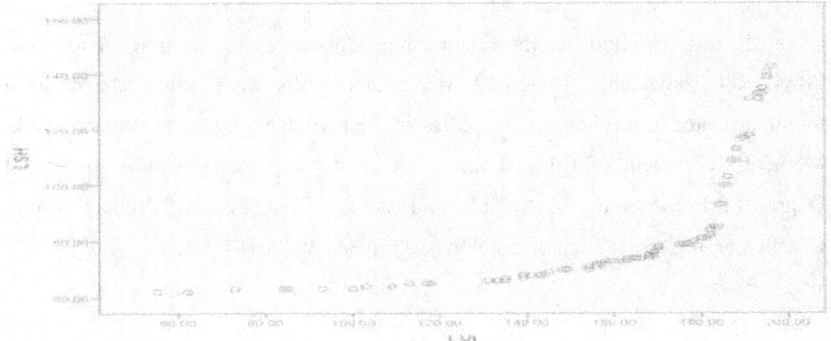

Objective 2: To ascertain the significance relationship between Vocational Interest and Socio-economic Status (Familial Variable) among Visually challenged adolescents.

The Second main objective of this study was to identify the relationship between Vocational Interest and Socio-economic Status (Familial Variable) of Visually Challenged Adolescents. So as to achieve this objective, the investigator frames the following null hypothesis for empirical verification

Hypothesis (Ho₂): There is no significant relationship between Vocational Interest and Socio-economic Status (Familial Variable) among Visually Challenged adolescents.

With the aim of find out the relationship between Vocational Interest and Socio-economic Status (Familial Variable) among Visually Challenged adolescents, the investigator first calculates the scores of the participant by using Pearson Product Moment Coefficient of Correlation for the total sample of 200. The table-4.5 represents Number of Sample, Degree of Freedom of the Sample and Value of the Pearson Product Moment Coefficient of Correlation along with its Significant Value (P- Value).

Table 4.5
Showing the relationship between Vocational Interest and Socio-economic Status (Familial Variable) among Visually Challenged Adolescents.

Variables	N	df	Calculated "r"	p- Value
Vocational Interest				
	200	198	.968**	.000
Socio-economic Status				

**Significant at 0.01 level of confidence (2 tailed)

The table 4.5 illustrates the intercorrelation between Vocational Interest and Socio-economic Status (Familial Variable) among Visually Challenged Adolescents for the total sample 200. The calculated coefficient values on the table 4.5 reveals that there is a positive and significant relationship between Vocational interest and Socio-economic Status. The Calculated Coefficient of Correlation (r- value) value for the total sample is .968 (P = .000) which is significant at 0.01 level of confidence. That means both variables (Vocational Interest & Study Socio-economic Status) are positively correlated which indicate the changed in values of one variable positively affect the other one. Therefore, the null hypothesis **"There is no significant relationship between Vocational Interest and Socio-economic Status (Familial Variable) among Visually Challenged adolescents"** is rejected.

Figure-4.4

Showing the Correlation between Vocational Interest and Socio-economic Status among Visually Challenged Adolescents

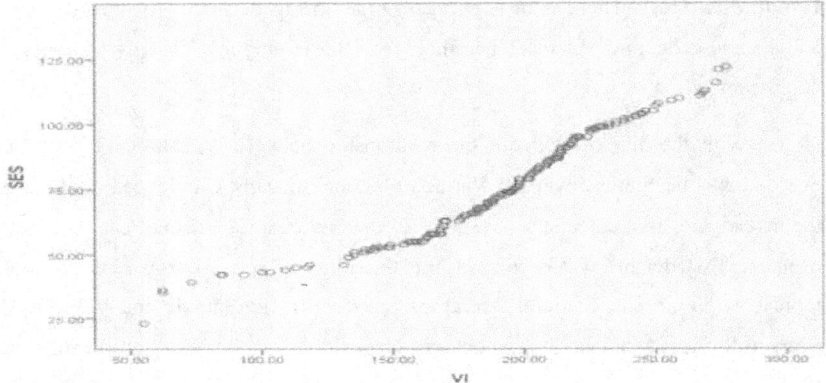

Objective 2.1: To ascertain the significance relationship between High Vocational Interest and High-level Socio-economic Status (Familial Variable) among Visually challenged adolescents.

The objective of this study was to identify the relationship between High Vocational Interest and High-level Socio-economic Status (Familial Variable) of Visually Challenged Adolescents. So as to achieve this objective, the investigator frames the following null hypothesis for empirical verification

Hypothesis (Ho$_{2.1}$): There is no significant relationship between High Vocational Interest and High-level Socio-economic Status (Familial Variable) among Visually Challenged adolescents.

In order to find out the relationship between High Vocational Interest and High-level Socio-economic Status (Familial Variable) among Visually Challenged adolescents, the investigator first calculates the scores of the participant by using

Pearson Product Moment Coefficient of Correlation for the selected sample of 100. The table-4.6 represents Number of Sample, Degree of Freedom of the Sample and Value of the Pearson Product Moment Coefficient of Correlation along with its Significant Value (P- Value).

Table 4.6

Showing the relationship between High Vocational Interest and High-level Socio-economic Status (Familial Variable) among Visually Challenged Adolescents.

Variables	N	Df	Calculated "r"	p- Value
High Vocational Interest				
	100	98	.981**	.000
High-level Socio-economic Status				

**Significant at 0.01 level of confidence (2 tailed)

The table 4.6 explore the intercorrelation between High Vocational Interest and High-level Socio-economic Status (Familial Variable) among Visually Challenged Adolescents for the selected sample of 100. The calculated coefficient values on the table 4.6 reveals that there is a positive and significant relationship between High Vocational interest and High-level Socio-economic Status. The Calculated Coefficient of Correlation (r- value) value is .981 (P = .000) which is significant at 0.01 level of confidence. That means both variables (High Vocational Interest & High-level Socio-economic Status) are positively correlated which indicate the changed in values of one variable positively affect the other one. Therefore, the null hypothesis **"There is no significant relationship between High Vocational Interest and High-level Socio-economic Status (Familial Variable) among Visually Challenged adolescents"** is rejected.

Figure-4.5
Showing the Correlation between High Vocational Interest and High-level Socio-economic Status among Visually Challenged Adolescents

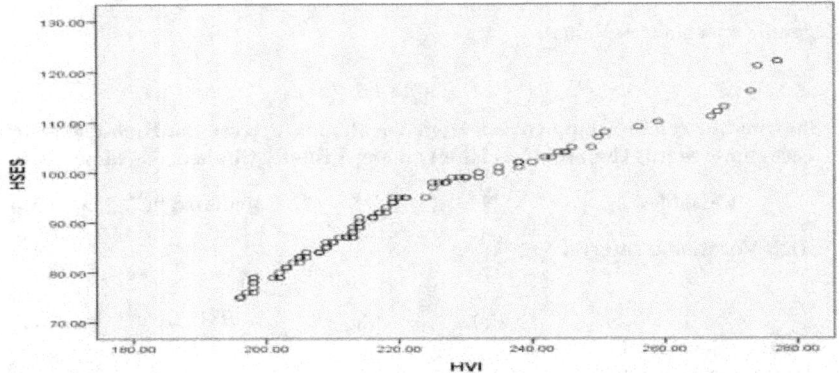

Objective 2.2: To ascertain the significance relationship between Low Vocational Interest and Low-level Socio-economic Status (Familial Variable) among Visually challenged adolescents.

This objective was to identify the relationship between Low Vocational Interest and Low-level Socio-economic Status (Familial Variable) of Visually Challenged Adolescents. So as to achieve this objective, the investigator frames the following null hypothesis for empirical verification

Hypothesis ($H_{02.2}$): There is no significant relationship between Low Vocational Interest and Low-level Socio-economic Status (Familial Variable) among Visually Challenged adolescents.

In order to find out the relationship between Low Vocational Interest and Low-level Socio-economic Status (Familial Variable) among Visually Challenged adolescents, the investigator first calculates the scores of the participant by using Pearson Product Moment Coefficient of Correlation for the selected sample of 100. The table-4.7 represents Number of Sample, Degree of Freedom of the Sample and Value of the Pearson Product Moment Coefficient of Correlation along with its Significant Value (P- Value).

Table 4.7

Showing the relationship between Low Vocational Interest and Low-level Socio-economic Status (Familial Variable) among Visually Challenged Adolescents.

Variables	N	df	Calculated "r"	p- Value
Low Vocational Interest	100	98	.960**	.000
Low-level Socio-economic Status				

**Significant at 0.01 level of confidence (2 tailed)

The table 4.7 shows the intercorrelation between Low Vocational Interest and Low-level Socio-economic Status (Familial Variable) among Visually Challenged Adolescents for the selected sample of 100. The calculated coefficient values on the table 4.7 reveals that there is a positive and significant relationship between Low Vocational interest and Low-level Socio-economic Status. The Calculated Coefficient of Correlation (r- value) value is .960 (P = .000) which is significant at 0.01 level of confidence. That means both variables (Low Vocational Interest & Low-level Socio-economic Status) are positively correlated which indicate the changed in values of one variable positively affect the other one. Therefore, the null hypothesis **"There is no significant relationship between Low Vocational Interest and Low-level Socio-economic Status (Familial Variable) among Visually Challenged adolescents"** is rejected.

Figure-4.6

Showing the Correlation between Low Vocational Interest and Low-level Socio-economic Status among Visually Challenged Adolescents

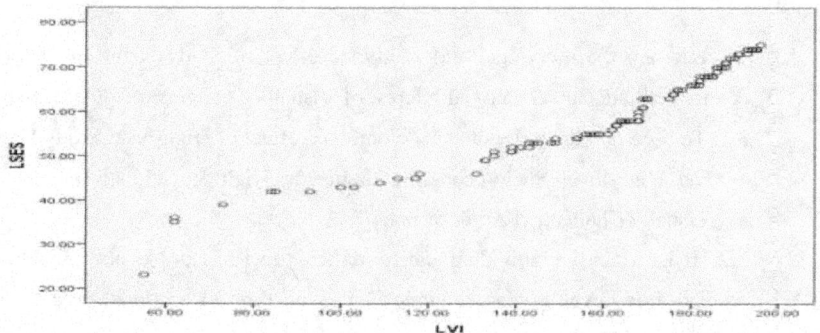

4.2. STUDY OF MULTIPLE REGRESSION ANALYSIS:

In statistics, regression analysis is a set of statistical processes for estimating the relationship between a dependent variable (outcome variable) and one or more independent variables (predictors). The most common form of regression analysis is linear regression, in which a researcher finds the line (or a more complex linear function) that most closely fits the data according to a specific mathematical criterion. Regression analysis is primarily used for two purposes. First, it is widely used for prediction and forecasting, where its use has substantial overlap with the field of machine learning. Second, in some situation's regression analysis can be used to infer causal relationship between the independent and dependent variables. Notably, regressions by themselves only reveal relationships between a dependent variable and a collection of independent variables in a fixed data set. To use regression for prediction or to infer causal relationships, respectively, a researcher must carefully justify why existing relationships have predictive power for a new context or why a relationship between two variables has a causal interpretation.

There are a number of approaches of regression analysis i.e. stepwise, backward, enter and forward. In this study investigator used enter approach to find out the effect of predictor variables (Study habit and Socio-economic Status) on the outcome variable (Vocational Interest). Statistical Package for Social Science (SPSS-22 Version) software used calculate reliable and authentic result to test various hypothesis and draw a conclusion on the basis of obtained data. In this study investigator used regression analysis for fond out the individual and combined effect on objective no 3. Which are presented below:

Objective:

3. To ascertain the individual and combined effect of Study Habit and Socio-economic Status on Vocational Interest of Visually Challenged Adolescents.
    3.1. To ascertain the individual and combined effect of High-level Study Habit and High-level Socio-economic Status on High Vocational Interest of Visually Challenged Adolescents.
    3.2. To ascertain the individual and combined effect of Low-level Study Habit and Low-level Socio-economic Status on Low Vocational Interest of Visually Challenged Adolescents.

Objective 3: To ascertain the individual and combined effect of Study Habit and Socio-economic Status on Vocational Interest of Visually Challenged Adolescents.

The third objective of this study is to determine the individual and combined effect of Study Habit and Socio-economic Status on Vocational Interest of Visually Challenged Adolescents. Therefore, to achieve this objective the investigator formulated the following null hypothesis for empirical verification.

Hypothesis (H_{03}): There is no individual and combined effect of Study Habit and Socio-economic Status on Vocational Interest of Visually Challenged Adolescents.

Thus, validate this hypothesis, the researcher treated the scores of Study Habit and Socio-economic Status on Vocational Interest for the sample of 200 using Simple Regression Analysis and the results and their interpretations are presented in table 4.8.

Table-4.8
Simple regression Analysis of Study Habit and Socio-economic Status on Vocational Interest of Visually Challenged Adolescents.

Independent Variables	Dependent Variable (Vocational Interest)			
	R- Value	R^2- Value	F- Value	Sig. Value
Study Habit	.977	.954	2044.651	.000
Socio-economic Status				

Dependent Variable: Vocational Interest
Predictors (Constant): Study Habit, socio-economic Status

Table 4.8 reveals that the calculated R and R^2 value are .977 and .954 respectively for the sample of 200. Thus, the combined effect of Study Habit and Socio-economic Status on Vocational Interest of Visually Challenged Adolescents is 95.4 percent and indicates that the fact 95.4 percent of variance of Study Habit and Socio-economic Status on Vocational Interest. The calculated F- value is 2044.651 which significant at 0.01 level of confidence and reveal that there is a significant combined effect of Study Habit and Socio-economic Status on Vocational Interest of Visually Challenged Adolescents.

Further, the investigator calculated individual effect of independent variables (Study Habit and Socio-economic Status) on Vocational Interest of Visually Challenged Adolescents. The table 4.9 reveals individual effect respectively:

Table: 4.9

Coefficients for Visually Challenged Adolescents

Model	Unstandardized Coefficient		Standardized Coefficient	t- value	Sig.
	B	Std. Error	Beta		
Constant	16.136	3.486	-	4.629	.000
Study Habit	-.355	.041	-.451	-8.692	.000
Socio-economic Status	2.922	.108	1.399	26.961	.000

Dependent Variable: Vocational Interest

The coefficient table 4.9 shows that Study Habit and Socio-economic Status have significant individual contribution on Vocational Interest of Visually Challenged Adolescents. The table 4.9 reveals that Study Habits has (Beta= -.451) 45.1 percent Negative influence on Vocational Interest of Visually Challenged Adolescents. That means the Beta value of Study Habit discloses that increase in Study Habit leads to 45.1 percent decrease in Vocational Interest of Visually Challenged Adolescents.

Whereas Socio-economic Status has positive influence on Vocational Interest of Visually Challenged Adolescents. The calculated Beta value is 1.399 which represents 139.9 percent significant positive influence on Vocational Interest. That means the Beta value of Socio-economic Status reveals that increase in Socio-economic Status leads to 139.9 percent increase in Vocational Interest of Visually Challenged Adolescents. Thus, the null hypothesis 3 **"There is no individual and combined effect of Study Habit and Socio-economic Status on Vocational Interest of Visually Challenged Adolescents"** is rejected.

Figure-4.7
Showing the individual and combined effect among Visually Challenged Adolescents

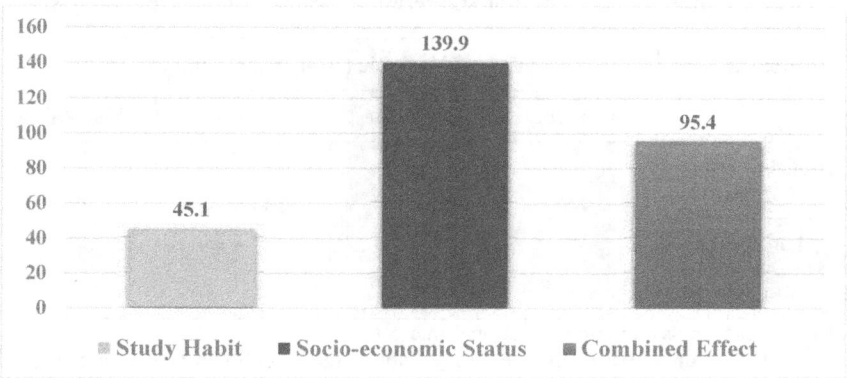

Objective 3.1: To ascertain the individual and combined effect of High-level Study Habit and High-level Socio-economic Status on High Vocational Interest of Visually Challenged Adolescents.

The objective of this study is to determine the individual and combined effect of High-level Study Habit and High-level Socio-economic Status on High Vocational Interest of Visually Challenged Adolescents. Therefore, to achieve this objective the investigator formulated the following null hypothesis for empirical verification.

Hypothesis ($H_{03.1}$): There is no individual and combined effect of High-level Study Habit and High-level Socio-economic Status on High Vocational Interest of Visually Challenged Adolescents.

Thus, validate this hypothesis, the researcher treated the scores of High-level Study Habit and High-level Socio-economic Status on High Vocational Interest for the sample of 100 using Simple Multiple Regression Analysis and the results and their interpretations are presented in table 4.10.

Table-4.10

Simple regression Analysis of High-level Study Habit and High-level Socio-economic Status on High Vocational Interest of Visually Challenged Adolescents.

Independent Variables	Dependent Variable (High Vocational Interest)			
	R- Value	R^2- Value	F- Value	Sig. Value
High-level Study Habit	.990	.979	2303.538	.000
High-level Socio-economic Status				

Dependent Variable: High Vocational Interest
Predictors (Constant): High-level Study Habit, High-level Socio-economic Status

Table 4.9 reveals that the calculated R and R^2 value are .990 and .979 respectively for the sample of 100. Thus, the combined effect of High-level Study Habit and High-level Socio-economic Status on High Vocational Interest of Visually Challenged Adolescents is 97.9 percent and indicates that the fact 97.9 percent of variance of High-level Study Habit and High-level Socio-economic Status on High Vocational Interest. The calculated F- value 2303.538 is significant at 0.01 level of confidence which reveal that there is a significant combined effect of High-level Study Habit and High-level Socio-economic Status on High Vocational Interest of Visually Challenged Adolescents.

Further, the investigator calculated individual effect of independent variables (High-level Study Habit and High-level Socio-economic Status) on High Vocational Interest of Visually Challenged Adolescents. The table 4.11 reveals individual effect respectively:

Table: 4.11
Coefficients for Visually Challenged Adolescents

Model	Unstandardized Coefficient		Standardized Coefficient	t- value	Sig.
	B	Std. Error	Beta		
Constant	78.953	3.709	-	21.288	.000
High-level Study Habit	-.502	.057	-.412	-8.847	.000
High-level Socio-economic Status	2.525	.086	1.372	29.483	.000

Dependent Variable: High Vocational Interest

The coefficient table 4.11 shows that High-level Study Habit and High-level Socio-economic Status have significant individual contribution on High Vocational Interest of Visually Challenged Adolescents. The value reveals that High-level Study Habits has (Beta= -.412) 41.2 percent Negative influence on Vocational Interest of Visually Challenged Adolescents. That means the Beta value of High-level Study Habit reveals that increase in High-level Study Habit leads to 41.2 percent decrease in High Vocational Interest of Visually Challenged Adolescents.

Whereas High-level Socio-economic Status has positive influence on High Vocational Interest of Visually Challenged Adolescents. The calculated Beta value is 1.372 which represents 137.2 percent significant positive influence on High Vocational Interest. That means the Beta value of High-level Socio-economic Status reveals that increase in High Socio-economic Status leads to 137.2 percent increase in High Vocational Interest of Visually Challenged Adolescents. Thus, the null hypothesis 3.1 **"There is no individual and combined effect of High-level Study Habit and High-level Socio-economic Status on High Vocational Interest of Visually Challenged Adolescents"** is rejected.

Figure-4.8

Showing the individual and combined effect among Visually Challenged Adolescents

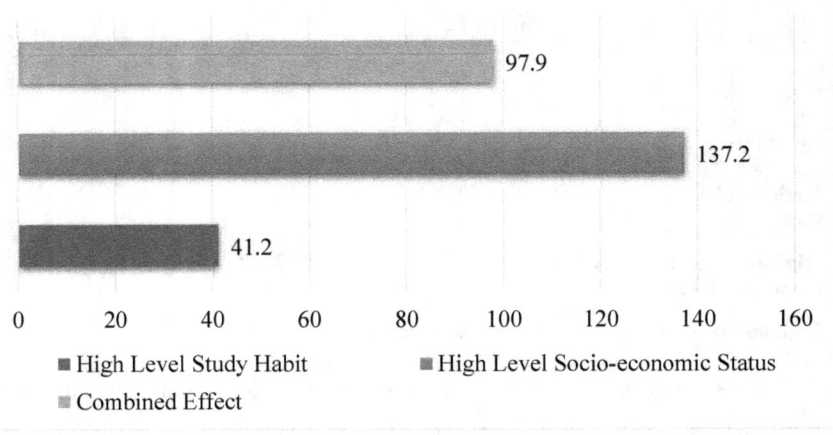

Objective 3.2: To ascertain the individual and combined effect of Low-level Study Habit and Low-level Socio-economic Status on Low Vocational Interest of Visually Challenged Adolescents.

The objective of this study is to determine the individual and combined effect of Low-level Study Habit and Low-level Socio-economic Status on Low Vocational Interest of Visually Challenged Adolescents. Therefore, to achieve this objective the investigator formulated the following null hypothesis for empirical verification.

Hypothesis ($H_{03.2}$): There is no individual and combined effect of Low-level Study Habit and Low-level Socio-economic Status on Low Vocational Interest of Visually Challenged Adolescents.

Thus, validate this hypothesis, the researcher treated the scores of Low-level Study Habit and Low-level Socio-economic Status on Low Vocational Interest for the sample of 100 using Simple Multiple Regression Analysis and the results and their interpretations are presented in table 4.12.

Table-4.12

Simple regression Analysis of Low-level Study Habit and Low-level Socio-economic Status on Low Vocational Interest of Visually Challenged Adolescents.

Independent Variables	Dependent Variable (High Vocational Interest)			
	R- Value	R^2- Value	F- Value	Sig. Value
Low-level Study Habit	.974	.949	909.208	.000
Low-level Socio-economic Status				

Dependent Variable: Low-level Vocational Interest
Predictors (Constant): Low-level Study Habit, Low-level Socio-economic Status

Table 4.12 reveals that the calculated R and R^2 value are .974 and .949 respectively for the sample of 100. Thus, the combined effect of Low-level Study Habit and Low-level Socio-economic Status on Low Vocational Interest of Visually Challenged Adolescents is 94.9 percent and indicates that the fact 94.9 percent of variance of Low-level Study Habit and Low-level Socio-economic Status or Low Vocational Interest. The calculated F- value 909.208 is significant at 0.01 level of confidence which reveal that there is a significant combined effect of Low-level Study Habit and Low-level Socio-economic Status on Low Vocational Interest of Visually Challenged Adolescents.

Further, the investigator calculated individual effect of independent variables (Low-level Study Habit and Low-level Socio-economic Status) on Low Vocational Interest of Visually Challenged Adolescents. The table 4.13 reveals individual effect respectively:

Table: 4.13
Coefficients for Visually Challenged Adolescents

Model	Unstandardized Coefficient		Standardized Coefficient	t- value	Sig.
	B	Std. Error	Beta		
Constant	23.521	4.392	-	-5.356	.000
Low-level Study Habit	-.408	.056	-.291	-7.236	.000
Low-level Socio-economic Status	3.668	.123	1.200	29.833	.000

Dependent Variable: Low Vocational Interest

The coefficient table 4.13 shows that Low-level Study Habit and Low-level Socio-economic Status have significant individual contribution on Low Vocational Interest of Visually Challenged Adolescents. The value reveals that Low-level Study Habit has (Beta= -.291) 29.1 percent Negative influence on Low Vocational Interest of Visually Challenged Adolescents. That means the Beta value of Low-level Study Habit reveals that increase in Low-level Study Habit leads to 29.1 percent decrease in Low Vocational Interest of Visually Challenged Adolescents.

Whereas Low-level Socio-economic Status has positive influence on Low Vocational Interest of Visually Challenged Adolescents. The calculated Beta value is 1.200 which represents 120 percent significant positive influence on Low Vocational Interest. That means the Beta value of Low-level Socio-economic Status reveals that increase in Low-level Socio-economic Status leads to 120 percent increase in Low-level Vocational Interest of Visually Challenged Adolescents. Thus, the null hypothesis 3.2 **"There is no individual and combined effect of Low-level Study Habit and Low-level Socio-economic Status on Low Vocational Interest of Visually Challenged Adolescents"** is rejected.

Figure-4.9

Showing the individual and combined effect among Visually Challenged Adolescents

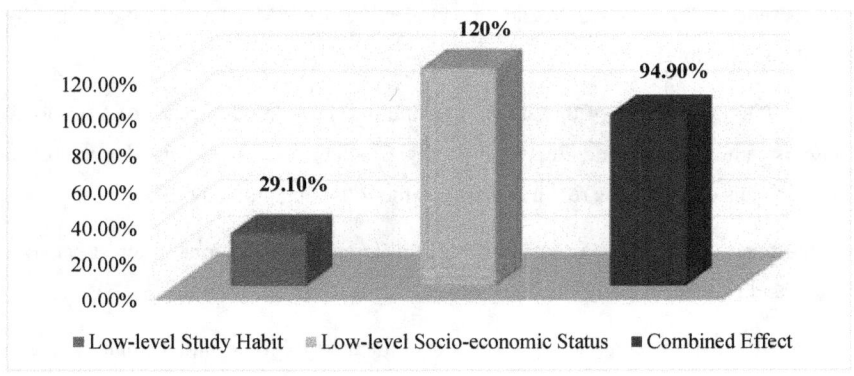

4.3 STUDY OF MEAN DIFFERENCES:

A mean is the most satisfactory measure for characterizing a group, it is most important here to determine whether the difference between means of sample is significant or not. A "t" test in statistics used to discover the mean difference between two groups when the variance of two acquire normal distributions are not known. In this study the investigator used a "t" test to know the significance difference in the mean score of Vocational Interest, Study Habit and Socio-economic status among all comparative groups under study. Objective 4 to 9 are:

Objective:

4. To compare Vocational Interest between Male and Female Visually Challenged Adolescents.
5. To compare Vocational Interest between Rural and Urban visually challenged adolescents.
6. To compare Study Habit between Male and Female Visually Challenged Adolescents.
7. To compare Study Habit between Rural and Urban visually challenged adolescents.
8. To compare Socio-economic Status between Male and Female visually challenged adolescents.

9. To compare Socio-economic Status between Rural and Urban visually challenged adolescents.

Objective 4: To compare Vocational Interest between Male and Female Visually Challenged Adolescents.

The objective-4 of this study is to find out the mean difference of Vocational Interest among Male and Female Visually Challenged Adolescents. Therefore, to validate this objective the researcher frames the following null hypothesis:

Hypothesis ($H_0 4$): There is no significance difference in Vocational Interest between Male and Female Visually Challenged Adolescents.

In order to compare the Vocational Interest of Male and Female Visually Challenged Adolescents "t" test applied. Therefore, the mean score, SD's, and "t"-values for Vocational Interest of Male and Female Visually Challenged Adolescents are given in below table 4.14.

Table-4.14

Showing mean difference in Vocational Interest between Male and Female Visually Challenged Adolescents (N=200)

Variable	Male Adolescents		Female Adolescents		df	t-Value	P- Value
	Mean	SD	Mean	SD	198	2.667*	.008
Vocational Interest	198.10	37.525	182.87	43.057			

* Significant at 0.05 level of Confidence (2- Tailed)

To find out the mean differences in Vocational Interest between Male and Female Visually Challenged Adolescents, researcher calculated the mean, SD, and "t" score of both the groups for the sample of 200 (100 Male and 100 Female). The mean and SD for Male Visually Challenged Adolescents were 198.10 and 37.525 while mean and SD for Female Visually Challenged Adolescents were 182.87 and 43.057 respectively. The calculated "t" value was 2.667 with its Significant value 0.008 (P-value) as shown on table 4.13. Therefore, it can be concluded that there was a significant mean difference in Vocational Interest between Male and Female Visually Challenged Adolescents. The calculated mean scores as shown on table 4.13 also indicate that the Vocational Interest of Male adolescents is higher than female Visually Challenged Adolescents. This finding was supported by the study of Yum

(1942) and Small (1955) who found a significance difference between male and female senior secondary students on vocational interest. Another study conducted by Monika (2014) who found that the female students have poor vocational interests, the reason may be to such extent that the female students are not equally exposed to educational opportunities like male once more. Some dissimilar findings also found by the investigator where the both group (Male and Female) shows similar interest towards vocation. The study conducted by Singh (2014), Edward and Quinter (2011), S.K. (2019) were dissimilar to this finding. The figure 4.10 also represents these above findings. Thus, the null hypothesis 4 **"There is no significance difference in Vocational Interest between Male and Female Visually Challenged Adolescents"** is rejected.

Table-4.10

Showing the mean difference in Vocational Interest between Male and Female Visually Challenged adolescents

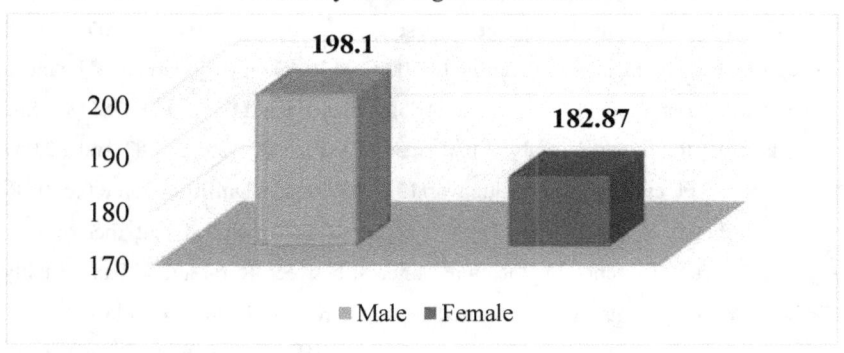

Objective 5: To compare Vocational Interest between Rural and Urban visually challenged adolescents.

The objective-5 of this study is to find out the mean difference of Vocational Interest among Rural and Urban Visually Challenged Adolescents. Therefore, to validate this objective the researcher frames the following null hypothesis:

Hypothesis 5: There is no significance difference in Vocational Interest between Rural and Urban Visually Challenged Adolescents.

In order to compare the Vocational Interest of Rural and Urban Visually Challenged Adolescents "t" test applied. Therefore, the mean score, SD's, and "t"-values for Vocational Interest of Rural and Urban Visually Challenged Adolescents are given in below table 4.15.

Table-4.15

Showing mean difference in Vocational Interest between Rural and Urban Visually Challenged Adolescents (N=200)

Variable	Rural Adolescents		Urban Adolescents		df	t-Value	P- Value
	Mean	SD	Mean	SD	198	15.802**	.000
Vocational Interest	219.58	18.543	159.83	32.954			

** Significant at 0.01 level of Confidence (2- Tailed)

To find out the mean differences in Vocational Interest between Rural and Urban Visually Challenged Adolescents, researcher calculated the mean, SD, and "t" score of both the groups for the sample of 200 (100 Rural and 100 Urban). The mean and SD for Rural Visually Challenged Adolescents were 219.58 and 18.543 while mean and SD for Urban Visually Challenged Adolescents were 159.83 and 32.954 respectively. The calculated "t" value was 15.802 with its Significant value 0.000 (P-value) as shown on table 4.14. Therefore, it can be concluded that there was a significant mean difference in Vocational Interest between Rural and Urban Visually Challenged Adolescents. The calculated mean scores as shown on table 4.14 also indicate that the Vocational Interest of Rural adolescents is higher than Urban Visually Challenged Adolescents. That means rural Visually Challenged Adolescents are more aware about their vocational interest than Urban Visually Challenged Adolescents. The figure 4.11 also represents these above findings. Thus, the null hypothesis 5 **"There is no significance difference in Vocational Interest between Rural and Urban Visually Challenged Adolescents"** is rejected.

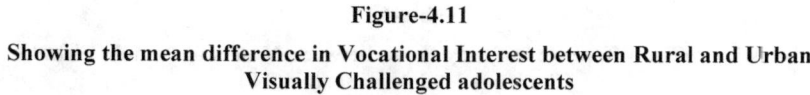

Figure-4.11

Showing the mean difference in Vocational Interest between Rural and Urban Visually Challenged adolescents

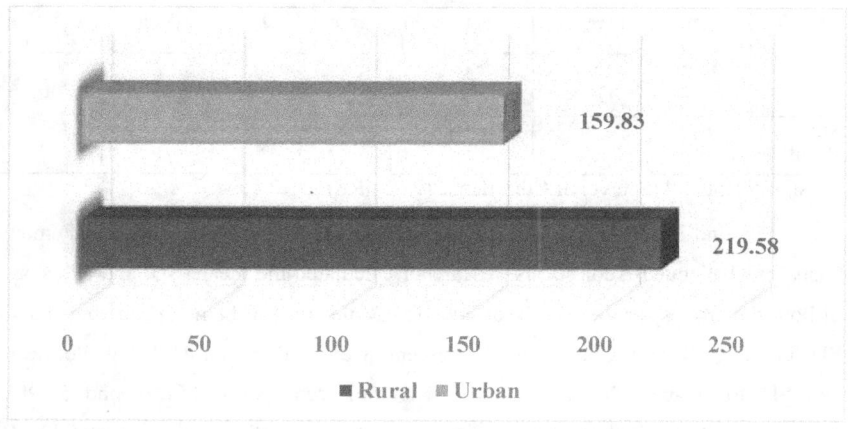

Objective 6: To compare Study Habit between Male and Female Visually Challenged Adolescents.

The objective-4 of this study is to find out the mean difference of Study Habit among Male and Female Visually Challenged Adolescents. Therefore, to validate this objective the researcher frames the following null hypothesis:

Hypothesis 6: There is no significance difference in Study Habit between Male and Female Visually Challenged Adolescents.

In order to compare the Study Habit of Male and Female Visually Challenged Adolescents "t" test applied. Therefore, the mean score, SD's, and "t"-values for Study Habit of Male and Female Visually Challenged Adolescents are given in below table 4.16.

Table-4.16

Showing mean difference in Study Habit between Male and Female Visually Challenged Adolescents (N=200)

Variable	Male Adolescents		Female Adolescents		df	t-Value	P- Value
	Mean	SD	Mean	SD	198	-6.692**	.000
Study Habit	110.35	41.777	154.98	51.986			

** Significant at 0.01 level of Confidence (2- Tailed)

To find out the mean differences in Study Habit between Male and Female Visually Challenged Adolescents, researcher calculated the mean, SD, and "t" score of both the groups for the sample of 200 (100 Male and 100 Female). The mean and SD for Male Visually Challenged Adolescents were 110.35 and 41.777 while mean and SD for Female Visually Challenged Adolescents were 154.98 and 51.986 respectively. The calculated "t" value was -6.692 with its Significant value 0.000 (P-value) as shown on table 4.16. Therefore, it can be concluded that there was a significant mean difference in Study Habit between Male and Female Visually Challenged Adolescents. The calculated mean scores as shown on table 4.16 also indicate that the Study Habit of Female adolescents is higher than Male Visually Challenged Adolescents. The figure 4.12 also represents these above findings. Thus, the null hypothesis **"There is no significance difference in Study Habit between Male and Female Visually Challenged Adolescents"** is rejected.

Figure-4.12

Showing the mean difference in Study Habit between Male and Female Visually Challenged adolescents

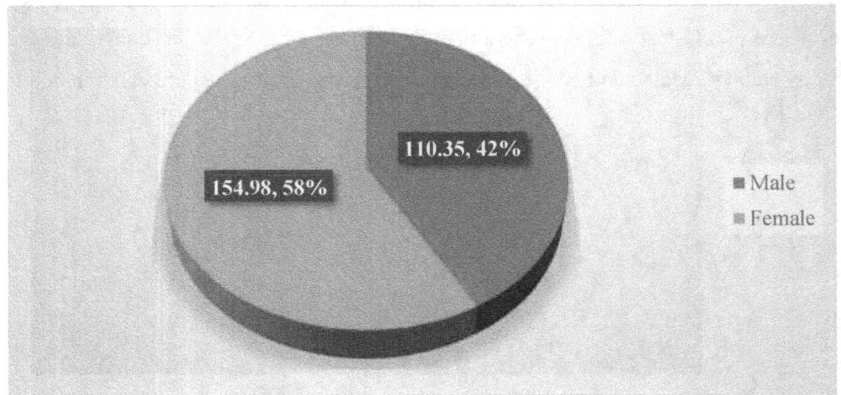

Objective 7: To compare Study Habit between Rural and Urban visually challenged adolescents.

The objective-7 of this study is to find out the mean difference of Study Habit among Rural and Urban Visually Challenged Adolescents. Therefore, to validate this objective the researcher frames the following null hypothesis:

Hypothesis 7: There is no significance difference in Study Habit between Rural and Urban Visually Challenged Adolescents.

In order to compare the Study Habit of Rural and Urban Visually Challenged Adolescents "t" test applied. Therefore, the mean score, SD's, and "t"-values for Socio-economic Status of Rural and Urban Visually Challenged Adolescents are given in below table 4.17

Table-4.17

Showing mean difference in Study Habit between Rural and Urban Visually Challenged Adolescents (N=200)

Variable	Rural Adolescents		Urban Adolescents		df	t-Value	P- Value
	Mean	SD	Mean	SD	198	17.447**	.000
Study Habit	92.34	35.172	173.61	30.539			

** Significant at 0.01 level of Confidence (2- Tailed)

To find out the mean differences in Study Habit between Rural and Urban Visually Challenged Adolescents, researcher calculated the mean, SD, and "t" score of both groups for the sample of 200 (100 Rural and 100 Urban). The calculated Mean and SD for Rural Visually Challenged Adolescents on the variable of Study Habit were 92.34 and 35.172 while mean and SD for Urban Visually Challenged Adolescents were 173.61 and 30.539 respectively. The calculated "t" value was 17.447 with its Significant value 0.000 (P- value) as shown on table 4.17. Therefore, it can be concluded that there was a significant mean difference in Study Habit between Rural and Urban Visually Challenged Adolescents. The calculated mean scores as shown on table 4.17 also indicate that the Study Habit of Urban Visually Challenged adolescents is higher than Rural Visually Challenged Adolescents. That means Urban Visually Challenged Adolescents have good Study Habit than Rural

Visually Challenged Adolescents. The figure 4.13 also represents these above findings. Thus, the null hypothesis 7 **"There is no significance difference in Study Habit between Rural and Urban Visually Challenged Adolescents"** is rejected.

Table-4.13

Showing the mean difference in Study Habit between Rural and Urban Visually Challenged adolescents

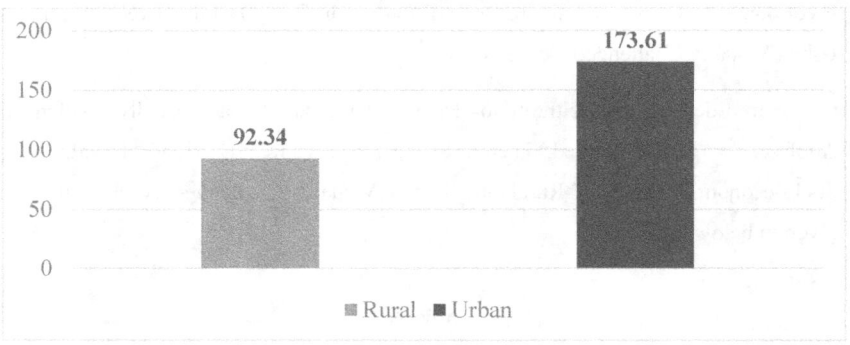

Objective 8: To compare Socio-economic Status between Male and Female visually challenged adolescents.

The objective-8 of this study is to find out the mean difference of Socio-economic Status among Male and Female Visually Challenged Adolescents. Therefore, to validate this objective the researcher frames the following null hypothesis:

Hypothesis 8: There is no significance difference in Socio-economic Status between Male and Female Visually Challenged Adolescents.

In order to compare the Socio-economic Status of Male and Female Visually Challenged Adolescents "t" test applied. Therefore, the mean score, SD's, and "t"-values for Study Habit of Male and Female Visually Challenged Adolescents are given in below table 4.18.

Table-4.18

Showing mean difference in Socio-economic Status between Male and Female Visually Challenged Adolescents (N=200)

Variable	Male Adolescents		Female Adolescents		df	t-Value	P- Value
	Mean	SD	Mean	SD	198	-6.127**	.000
Study Habit	67.97	21.256	83.60	14.108			

** Significant at 0.01 level of Confidence (2- Tailed)

To find out the mean differences in Socio-economic Status between Male and Female Visually Challenged Adolescents, researcher calculated the mean, SD, and "t" score of both the groups for the sample of 200 (100 Male and 100 Female). The mean and SD for Male Visually Challenged Adolescents were 67.97 and 21.256 while mean and SD for Female Visually Challenged Adolescents were 83.60 and 14.108 respectively. The calculated "t" value was -6.127 with its Significant value 0.000 (P-value) as shown on table 4.18. Therefore, it can be concluded that there was a significant mean difference in Socio-economic Status between Male and Female Visually Challenged Adolescents. The calculated mean scores as shown on table 4.18 also indicate that the Socio-economic Status of Female adolescents is higher than Male Visually Challenged Adolescents. The figure 4.14 also represents these above findings. Thus, the null hypothesis 8 **"There is no significance difference in Socio-economic Status between Male and Female Visually Challenged Adolescents"** is rejected.

Table-4.14

Showing the mean difference in Socio-economic Status between Male and Female Visually Challenged adolescents

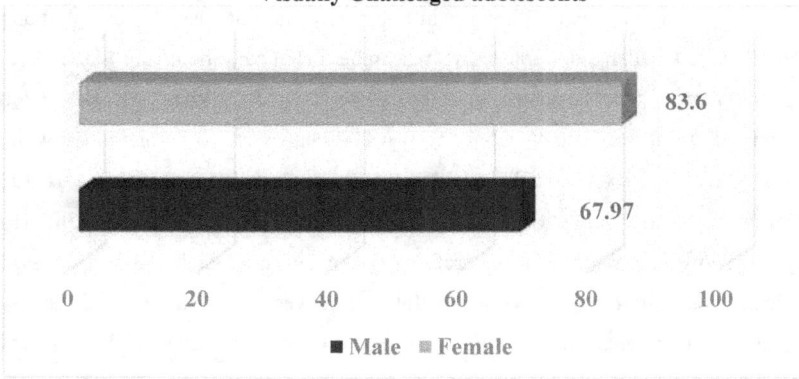

Objective 9: To compare Socio-economic Status between Rural and Urban visually challenged adolescents.

The objective-9 of this study is to find out the mean difference of Socio-economic Status among Rural and Urban Visually Challenged Adolescents. Therefore, to validate this objective the researcher frames the following null hypothesis:

Hypothesis 8: There is no significance difference in Socio-economic Status between Rural and Urban Visually Challenged Adolescents.

In order to compare the Socio-economic Status of Rural and Urban Visually Challenged Adolescents "t" test applied. Therefore, the mean score, SD's, and "t"-values for Socio-economic Status of Rural and Urban Visually Challenged Adolescents are given in below table 4.19.

Table-4.19

Showing mean difference in Socio-economic Status between Rural and Urban Visually Challenged Adolescents (N=200)

Variable	Rural Adolescents		Urban Adolescents		df	t-Value	P- Value
	Mean	SD	Mean	SD	198	13.304**	.000
Socio-economic Status	61.44	9.610	89.06	18.402			

** Significant at 0.01 level of Confidence (2- Tailed)

To find out the mean differences in Socio-economic Status between Rural and Urban Visually Challenged Adolescents, researcher calculated the mean, SD, and "t" score of both groups for the sample of 200 (100 Rural and 100 Urban). The calculated Mean and SD for Rural Visually Challenged Adolescents were 61.44 and 9.610 while mean and SD for Urban Visually Challenged Adolescents were 89.06 and 18.402 respectively. The calculated "t" value was 13.304 with its Significant value 0.000 (P-value) as shown on table 4.19. Therefore, it can be concluded that there was a significant mean difference in Vocational Interest between Rural and Urban Visually Challenged Adolescents on the variable of Socio-economic Status. The calculated mean scores as shown on table 4.19 also indicate that the Socio-economic Status of

Urban Visually Challenged adolescents is higher than Rural Visually Challenged Adolescents. That means Urban Visually Challenged Adolescents were belong to good socio-economic family than Rural Visually Challenged Adolescents. The figure 4.15 also represents these above findings. Thus, the null hypothesis 9 **"There is no significance difference in Socio-economic Status between Rural and Urban Visually Challenged Adolescents"** is rejected.

Table-4.15

Showing the mean difference in Socio-economic Status between Rural and Urban Visually Challenged adolescents

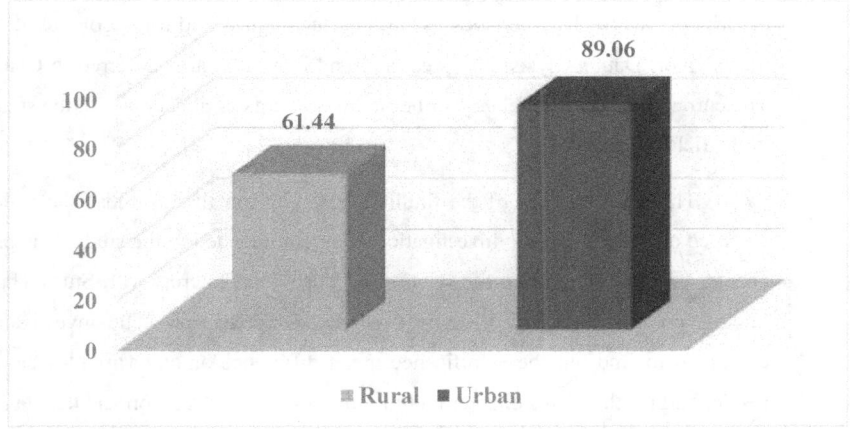

Chapter 5

FINDINGS, EDUCATIONAL IMPLICATIONS, AND SUGGESTIONS

The previous four chapters include the details regarding methodology that followed by the investigator in conducting the study. The Chapter- 1 contains all the theoretical and research context of the problem under the investigation. In Chapter- 2 the problem was precisely described. Chapter-3 defined the population and its proper description with characteristics, sampling technique, and the tools used by the investigator. Data analysis, interpretation, and its results are conferred in Chapter- 4. The current chapter is is related to the findings and its implication with the suggestion in the field of education.

The main purpose of the findings is to confirm that all those facts that have emerged as an result of the investigation are recommended in the study. The previous chapter precisely described the relation of Vocational Interest with Study Habit and Socio-economic Status of Visually Challenged Adolescents. The investigator also attempted to find out the significance mean difference among variables along with gender and locality. This chapter includes the findings, suggestion and the educational implication.

5.1. FINDINGS:

The present study leads to the following findings:

1. The vocational interest of visually challenged adolescents significantly correlated with study habit (Personal variable). However, its correlation with study habit is positive. This shows that high vocational interest always leads to high study habit among visually challenged adolescents.

2. When the investigator tries to find out the relationship between High Vocational Interest and High Study Habit of visually challenged adolescents and a significant and positive correlation was found. That means high vocational interest always goes with high study habit.

3. A significant and positive correlation also found between Low vocational Interest and Low-Level Study Habit of visually challenged adolescents. That means bad study habit always lead low level vocational interest.

4. The familial variable Socio-economic Status significantly and positively correlated with vocational interest of visually challenged adolescents. Those students having good vocational interest belongs to good socio-economic family.

5. When the investigator correlates High vocational interest and high-level socio-economic status of visually challenged adolescents a significant correlation was found. Correlation was positive.

6. A significant and positive correlation was found between low vocational interest and low-level socio-economic status of visually challenged adolescents. That means bad socio-economic status always lead low vocational interest.

7. The combined and individual effect of Study Habit and Socio-economic Status on Vocational Interest of Visually Challenged adolescents were measured. A significant positive combined effect was found on vocational interest. But, while measured effect individually, a negative significant effect of study habit and a positive significant effect of socio-economic status on vocational interest were reveal.

8. The investigator also calculated combined and individual effect of High-level Study Habit and High-level Socio-economic Status on High Vocational Interest of Visually Challenged adolescents and a significant positive combined effect was found on High Vocational Interest. But, while measured effect individually, a negative significant effect of High-level Study Habit and a positive significant effect of High-level Socio-economic Status on High Vocational Interest were found.

9. While measured the combined and individual effect of Low-level Study Habit and Low-level Socio-economic Status on Low Vocational Interest of Visually Challenged adolescents and a significant positive combined effect was found on Low Vocational Interest. When effect measured individually, a negative significant effect of Low-level Study Habit and a positive significant effect of Low-level Socio-economic Status on Low Vocational Interest were elicited.

10. In general, a significant difference was found in Vocational Interest among Visually Challenged Adolescents. It was found that Vocational Interest of Male Visually Challenged Adolescents is higher than Female Visually Challenged Adolescents. This shows that Female Visually Challenged Adolescents were unaware about their vocation. This finding favours the myth of society that female has to remain in home to do housewife job and male have to go outside for job to earn their living.

11. A significance difference also found in Vocational Interest of Rural and Urban Visually Challenged Adolescents. It was found that those Visually Challenged Adolescents belong to Rural area more aware regarding their vocation than the Urban Visually Challenged Students.

12. On the Study Habit variable significance difference was found between Male and Female Visually Challenged Adolescents. Study habit of Female Visually Challenge Adolescents were good than Male Visually Challenged Adolescents.

13. A significance difference was found in Study Habit between Rural and Urban visually Challenged Adolescents. Study Habit of Urban Visually Challenge Adolescents are god than Rural Visually Challenge Adolescents.

14. While the investigator compares the mean difference on the variable of Socio-economic Status of Visually Challenge Adolescents a significance difference was confined. Socio-economic status of female Visually Challenge Adolescents is better than the male Visually Challenge Adolescents.

15. It was found a significance difference in Socio-economic Status of Visually Challenge Adolescents. Socio-economic status of Urban Visually Challenge Adolescents was better than Rural Visually Challenge Adolescents.

5.2 IMPLICATIONS:

On the basis of the findings the present study the investigator can point out following educational implications for teacher, parents and carrer counselor:

1. It was found by the investigator that Vocational interest of visually challenged adolescents positively correlated with Study Habit. That mean by modifying study habit we can increase the vocational interest of visually challenged adolescents. Thus, it is the responsibility of the parents, guardians and teacher to

help the student in shaping a good study habit so that the vocational interest of visually challenged adolescents will be substantial according to their capability.

2. In this study it was also found by the investigator that socio-economic status of visually challenged adolescents positively correlated with vocational interest. It means if family condition or socio-economic status of the family of visually challenged adolescents improved than automatically develop the vocational interest. Thus, the government of the state or central should make some policies for their people which will increase the family earning.

3. Study Habit and Socio-economic Status both have a strong influence on vocational interest of visually challenged adolescents. This type of study is will be very helpful for teacher, parents and guidance counsellor in predicting their vocation for future life.

4. The study also made an effort to find out the difference in vocational interest between male and female visually challenged adolescents. Male visually challenged adolescents show better vocational interest than female. Thus, it is the responsibility of the teacher, parents and career counsellor to motive the students and make available information regarding jobs so that the discrimination in interest will overcome.

5. It was also found by the investigator that rural visually challenged adolescents are more aware than urban adolescents. Thus, parents, teacher and local authority should take possible step to develop vocational interest among urban visually challenged adolescents.

6. Female visually challenged adolescents possesses good study habit than male adolescents. Urban visually challenged adolescents also show good study habit than rural adolescents. Parents, local guardians and teacher should modify study habit by providing good leaning environment among male and rural visually adolescents.

7. Finally, in the case of Socio-economic status female visually challenged adolescents have good socio-economic condition than male adolescents. Urban visually challenged adolescents also have better family condition than rural adolescents. Socio-economic status has significant role in developing vocational

interest among students. Therefore, the findings of the will be very helpful for teacher, career counselor in determining interest among students.

5.3. THE SUGGESTIONS FOR FURTHER RESEARCH:

Some suggestions related to this study for further research are given below:

1. The present study conducted only on 200 visually challenged adolescents. Therefore, a similar study can be conducted with a large sample (estimated 800 to 1000) in a large geographical area to get more authentic and reliable generalizations.

2. The study carried out on visually challenged adolescents of Aligarh district. These findings are not generalized on all visually challenged adolescents thorough out the country. A similar study can be conducted by the investigator on normal adolescents whom studying in different government and private school.

3. In this study only measure the relationship and effect of independent variables (Study Habit and Socio-economic Status) on dependent variable (Vocational Interest). There are lots of factors that affect vocational interest. By selecting those factors, a fresh study can be conducted.

4. The study used correlation of coefficients, Regression analysis and t-test. Another research can be conducted by applying different methodology.

5. Finally, the study conducted only on selected visually challenged adolescents. Thus, this finding of the study was delimited only to visually challenged adolescents of Aligarh district. This is not applicable for all the adolescent.

REFERENCES

Afrin, S. (2015). A comparative study of self-concept, personality traits, intelligence, aspiration level and vocational interest, among boys and girls at secondary school level. Ph.D. thesis. Department of Education. AMU. Aligarh.

Agarwal, Rashmi, Indrakumar (2014) "Role of Vocational Education in Shaping Socio-Economic Landscape in India". Indian Journal of Industrial Relations, Vol. 49, No. 3, Special Issue on Skill Development (Jan. 2014) pp. 483-498.

Aggarwal, J. C. (2008). Modern Indian education (4th ed.). Shipra publications. Delhi-110092 (India).

Aggarwal, J. C. (7th edition, Reprint 2013), 'Landmarks in the History of Modern Indian Education', Vikas Publishing House Pvt. Ltd. E-28, Sector-8, Noida-201301(UP), (ISBN- 9788125937180), P- 43

Ahsan, Q.M G. and Ahmmod, S.M M. (2005) . Analyzing Study Habits of Distance Learners: A Case Study of Bangladesh Open University. Indian Journal of Open Learning 14 (1).

Akhter, Z. (2008) Impact Study of SSC and HSC Students of the Open School of Bangladesh Open University. Indian Journal of Open Learning 17(2).

Alam, M.M. (2001) studied. "Academic Achievement in relation to socio-economic status, Anxiety level and Achievement Motivation: A comparative study of Muslim and Non-Muslim School Children of U.P." Ph.D. Thesis.

Ali, M. (1998). Personal Values, career aspirations, academic achievement and socio-economic status as determinants of educational choice at senior secondary level. Ph.D. Thesis. Department of Education. AMU. Aligarh.

Allport, G. W. (1961). Patterns and growth in personality. New York: Holt,

Allport, G.W. (1937). Personality: A Psychological Interpretation. New York: Holt, Rinehart and Winston.

References

Arora, P.N. et al. (1988). "Educational and vocational aspirations of students of class XII perception of an interview schedule." Perceptive in educational research, 55(6), 47.

Arya, P. P. (Ed., 2006). Higher Education and Global Challenges, Systems and Opportunities, Deep and Deep Publication Pvt .Ltd. New Delhi , 152

Bayti, J.L. (1970). Vocational Preferences of secondary schools learners. Rajasthan board journal of education, 2(4), 7-42.

Best J.W and Khan J (1992). Research in Education (6th edition) New Delhi Prentice Hall of India Pvt. Ltd.

Best, J.W. (2004). Research in Education. New Delhi: Prentice Hall of India Private Ltd.

Best, J.W. Kahn (2012). Research in Education. New Delhi: Prentice Hall of India Private Ltd. P. 365.

Best, J.W. Kahn (2012). Research in Education. New Delhi: Prentice Hall of India Private Ltd. P. 356.

Best, J.W., (1970). Research in Education. New Delhi, Prentice Hall of India Private Limited.

Best, John & Prentice, W. (1978).Research in Education, New Delhi: Hall of India

Bhargava, M. & Arora, Saroj (Ed.) (2001). Parental Behavior; Agra : H.P. Bhargava Book House

Bhargava, M. & Arora, Saroj (ed.) (2004). Human Behavior and organizational excellence. Delhi: Sunrise Publications.

Bhargava, M. & Qureshi, A.N. (2000). Psychological preparedness for career competence. The Counselor. Alwar: Centre for Psychological Testing, Counseling, Management studies and research, p. 41-42.

Bhargava, M. & Sharma, A. (1995). Scholastic attainment and career maturity. Indian Journal of Psychometry and Education, 26(1), 25-30.

Bhargava, M. (1994). Relevance of Psychology for Vocationalisation at +2 stage. Education in Asia, 14 (2-3), 60-62.

Bhargava, M. (2000). Modern Psychological Testing and Measurement. (12th End.) Hindi, Agra: H.P. Bhargava Book House.

Bilos, A and Turkalj, D. (2017). Mobile learning usage and preferences of vocational secondary school students: the cases of Austria, the Czech Republic, and Germany. Our economy, vol. 63, no. 1, pp 59-69.

Bilos, A; Turkalj, D; & Kelić, I. (2017). Mobile Learning Usage and Preferences of Vocational Secondary School Students: The cases of Austria, the Czech Republic, and Germany. NaseGospodarstvo/ Our Economy, 63(1), pp. 59-69

Biswas, P.K and Mythili, G. (2004) .Impact of Distance Education Programmes of IGNOU on Personal and Career Development of Distance Learners. Indian Journal of Open Learning. 13,(1).

Bland, j. M.; Altman, D. G. (1996) Statistics notes: measurement error. BMJ. 312 (7047): 1654.

Boggiano, A.K. Main D.S and Katz P.A. (1990). Children's Preference for Challenge. The role of perceived competence and control. Journal of Personality and Social Psychology, 54, 134-141.

Borchert, M.T. (2002). "Career choice factors of High School Students: A Research Paper." The Graduate College University of Wisconsin Stout.

Borg, W. R., & Gall, M. D. (1989). Educational research. An introduction (5th Ed.). White Plains, NY: Longman.

Bourzgui, F; Abidine, Z; Serhier, Z; Samir Dioun, S; & Othmani, M.B. (2014). Motivational Factors Influencing Career Choices of Moroccan Dental Students. OHDM - Vol. 13 - No. 2

Brook, J.S. Whiteman et al. (1996). "Aspiration levels of and for children: Age, sex, race, socio-economic correlates." Journal of Genetic Psychology 121(1), 3-16.

Bruce et.al. (2017). Motivation for occupational preference among students of Regional Maritime University in Nungua, ACCRA-Ghana. International Journal of Research- Granthaalayah, vol.5 (Issue 8).

Buch, M.B., (1983). Fourth Survey of Educational Research, New Delhi. N.C.E.R.T.

Buch, M.B., (1987). Third Survey of Educational Research, New Delhi N.C.E.R.T.

Camp and Rothnay, J.W. (1970). "Parental response to counsellor's suggestions." School Counsellor (3), (200-203).

Chandra, Sunanda (1990). "Self Concept, Parental Influence, SES, and Sex ini relation to career choice attitudes among High School Students." Indian Educational Review, Vol. XXV, No. 1, August.

Chaudhari V.S., Vaidya S., Navalakha N.G., and Mahapatra, B.C. (1998). Effect of teaching strategies and socio-economic status on self-concept of the learner, Indian Psychological Review, 50 (4): 216-223.

Chauhan A, Chocha R. (2017) A Psychological Study of Vocational Interest among Secondary Students. International Journal of Indian Psychology, Volume 4, (3), pp. 113-120 DIP: 18.01.091/20170403

Chauhan Dr. C. P. S. (2004). 'Modern Indian Education Policies, Progress and Problem', Kanishka Publisher, Distributors 4697/5-21A, Ansari Road, Daryaganj, New Delhi-110002, (ISBN- 8173916160), Pp- 125-126

Chauhan Dr. C. P. S. (2004). 'Modern Indian Education Policies, Progress and Problem', Kanishka Publisher, distributors 4697/5-21A, Ansari Road, Daryaganj, New Delhi- 110002, (ISBN- 8173916160), Pp- 2-3

Chauhan, C. P. S. (2004). Modern Indian education: Policies, progress and problems. Kanishka Publishers.

Chauhan, S. S. (1978). Advanced Educational Psychology, Psychology of Adjustment. Vikas Publishing House Pvt. Ltd. P-410-411.

Chauhan, S.S. (1996). "The general content of life; implications for socio-economic status in men's career life plans." Career development quarterly 41, 227-237.

Cherry, N. (1974): Components of occupational Interest. The British Journal of Education and Psychology, 44.

Chopra, S.L. (1984). "Socio-economic background and occupational aspirations." Indian Educational Review, XIX(1), 99-105.

References

Chuang, Ning-Huang et al. (2009). "Student Perception of career choices: The impact of Academic Major." Journal of Family and Consumer Science Education, Vol. 27, Issue 2, pp. 10-20.

Clealeck, Edward, T. (2007). "Culturally disadvantaged boys and girls aspirations to and knowledge of white-collar and professional occupations." Urban Education, 1(3), 164-174.

Cooper, H.M. (1989). Integrating Research: A Guide for Literature Reviews. 2nd Ed., Sage Publications, Newbury Park, California.

Crites, John O. (1969). Vocational Psychology. The Study of Vocational Behaviour and Development, New York: McGraw-Hill Book Co.

Dabir, O. (1986). "A study of vocational aspirations as a function of aptitudes and motivational patterns among the boys and girls studying in class IX, X, XI grades in Nagpur district." IV Survey of Research in Education, 1, 529-530.

Daing, S. Ahmad (2012), "Career preference at higher secondary level in relation to gender, academic streams and academic level – A study.

Daniel, B; & Ahima, Q.F. (2017). Motivation for occupational preference among students of regional Maritime University in Nungua, Accra. International Journal of Research – granthaalayah, 5(8), pp. 158-174, ISSN: 2350-0530(O), ISSN- 2394-3629(P)

David, Yerkes (1989). Webster's Dictionary of the English Language. New Jersey: Gramercy Books.

Department of Psychology, University of British Columbia (2007). Impact of Socioeconomic Status on Physiological Health in Adolescents: an Experimental Manipulation of Psychosocial Factors, Vancouver, British Columbia, Canada.

Dodge, Y. (2003). The Oxford Dictionary of Statistical Terms. OUP. ISBN 0-19-850994-4.

Duncan, G.J.: Day, M.C.; McDonough, P. and Williams, D. R. (2002). Optimal indicators of socio-economic status for health research. American Journal of Public Health, 92, 1151-1157.

Dunne et al. (2011). "Sex Differences in the Educational and occupational Aspirations of Rural Youth." Journal of Vocational Behaviour, 18(1): 56-66.

Edwards, K & Quinter, M. (2011). Factors Influencing Students Career Choices among Secondary School students in Kisumu Municipality, Kenya. Journal of Emerging Trends in Educational Research and Policy Studies (JETERAPS,) 2 (2): pp. 81-87

Edwards, K. & Quinter, M. (2011). "Factors influencing students career choice among secondary school students in Kisumu Municipality, Kanya." Journal of Emerging Trends in Educational Research and Policy Studies (2012): 81-87.

Elliott, A.C., & Woodward, W.A. (2007). Statistical analysis quick reference guidebook with SPSS examples. 1st ed. London: Sage Publications; 2007.

Empey, L. T. (1956). Social Class and Occupational Aspiration: A Comparison of absolute and realistic measurement. American Sociological Review, 1956, 21, pp. 703-709

Empey, L.T. (2004). "Social Class and Occupational Aspiration – A comparison of Absolute and Relative Measurement." American Sociological Review, 21, 703-709.

Eremie, M.D. (2015). Comparative Analysis of Factors Influencing Career Choices among Senior Secondary School Students in Rivers State, Nigeria. Arabian Journal of Business and Management Review, 5(1), pp. 1-3

Eremie, M.D. (2015). Comparative analysis of factors influencing career choices among senior secondary school students in Rivers State, Nigeria. Arabian journal of business and management review, 5, 1.

Esskinger, C.W. (1980). "Educational and Occupation aspirations and expectations and the educational, personal, and family characteristics of selected twelfth grade female students." Dissertation Abstracts International, 37(1-A), 255.

Esters, L.T., & Brown, S.E. (2005). "Factors Influencing Career Choices of Urban Agricultural Education." Journal of Agricultural Education, Vol. 47, No. 2.

References

Eyo, M. B. & Edet, P. B. (2011). Gender and Occupational Preferences among Senior High School Students in Cross River State Nigeria. African Research Review, 5(1), serial no. 18, pp. 327-341

Eyo, M.B. and Edet, P.B. (2011). Gender and Occupational Preferences among Senior High School Students in Cross River State Nigeria. An International Multi-Disciplinary Journal, Ethiopia. Vol. 5 (1), Serial No. 18, January, 2011 ISSN 1994-9057 (Print) ISSN 2070-0083 (Online) page no.327-341.

Faaz, M. & Ali, M. I. (2017). Study habits as a measure of academic achievement of senior secondary school students in relation to type of school and Gender. International Education & Research Journal, Vol. 3, Issue 6, pp-174.

Farkhanda Ahmar, Ehtesham Anwar (2013) "Socio Economic status and its relation to academic achievement of Higher Secondary School Students. IOSR Journal of Humanities and Social Science (IOSR-JHSS), Volume 13, Issue 3 (Jul-Aug. 2013), pp. 13-20.

Femi, A. and others (2010). Learners' Choice and Perception of Distance Learning Degree Programme of the National Open University of Nigeria. 19(1).

Field, A. (2009). Discovering statistics using SPSS. 3 ed. London: SAGE publications Ltd; 2009. p. 822.

Forer, B. R. (1953). Personality factors in occupational choice. Educational and Psychological Measurement. 13, pp. 361-366.

Forer, B.B. (1953). 'Personality Factors in Occupational Choices', Edu. Psychol. Measnt. 13, 361-366.

Forer, B.B. (1953): Personality Factors in Occupational Choice. Educational Psychology and Measurement, 13, 361-366.

Fouad, N.A. et al. (2016). Family Influence on Career Decision Making: Validation in India and the U.S. journal of career assessment, vol. 24(1), 197-212.

Fouad, N.A; Kim, S.; Ghosh, A.; Chang, W, & Fiueiredo, C. (2015). Family Influence on Career Decision Making: Validation in India and the United States, Journal of Career Assessment, 24(1), pp. 197-212

Gaikwad, et al. (2012) "Career preferences and attitude towards the rural health services among the graduating interns of a medical college in Bangalore." International Journal of Biological & Media Research, 3(2), 2012, pp. 1577-1580

Gati, Itamer (1993): Career compromises. Journal of Counseling Psychology. Vol. 40(4), 416-424.

Gaur, J.S. (1974): the effect of level of intelligence on the occupational aspiration of the higher secondary schools students in Delhi. Indian Journal of psychology, (Jan) 49(2), 139-148.

Gaur, V. (2012). A study of classroom morale of senior secondary school students in relation to their socio-economic status, lows of control and intelligence. Doctoral thesis (Education). Maharishi Dayanand University. Rohtak.

Gesinde, A.M. A study of vocational preference of hearing-Impaired students. A Publication of National Resource Centre for the Disabled, pp. 126-131

Ghosh, Suresh C. (2007). 'History of Education in India', Published by Prem Rawat Publications, Satyam Apts, Sector 3, Jawahar Nagar, Jaipur 302004 (India), (ISBN – 8131601617), P- 454

Ginzberg (1952): Toward a theory of occupational choice. Occupations, 30, 491-494.

Ginzberg (1999). 'Towards a Theory of Occupational Choice', Occupations, 30, 491-494.

Glanakos, Irene (1999): Patterns of Career Choice of Career decision making and self efficacy. Journal of vocational behavior, vol. 54(2), 244-258.

Gomez, B. (2010). "Relationship between gender, parenting and adolescent occupational aspiration." Personal and Guidance Journal, 42, 558-563.

Good, C.V. (1959). Introduction to Educational Research. New York: Appleton century, Craft No.1.

Goon, A.M. , Gupta , M.K. AND Dasgupta, B., Fundamentals of Statistics(1&2)

Grace, Bennet (2011). The Relationship of mental ability to occupational choice of adults." Vocational guidance magazine, 10, 354, 358.

Gresham, Mary Harley (1995). "Occupational Aspiration Expectation Congruence and Self Efficacy in Career Decision making." Dissertation Abstracts International, 53(12), 4209-A.

Grewal (1974). Vocational environment and educational and occupational choices. Third survey of research in education, Ed. M.B. Buch, NCERT, New Delhi.

Grewal, J.S. (1976). "Occupational Aspiration and Socio-economic study of advantaged and disadvantaged high school students." Agra: National Psychological Corporation.

Guilford J P& Frucher B: Fundamental Statistics in Psychology and Education. International Students Edition, New Delhi, Inc.1978.

Guilford, J.P. (1954). Psychometric Methods, (2nd ed.), New York : McGraw-Hill.

Guilford, J.P. (1956). Fundamental statistics in Psychology and Education, McGraw-Hill Book Company, INC.

Gupta (2007), 'Education in India', KSK Publisher and Distributions, 7/26, L.G.F., Ansari Road, Darya Ganj, New Delhi-2, (ISBM- 8190461757), P- 42

Gupta (2007), 'Education in India', KSK Publisher and Distributions, 7/26, L.G.F., Ansari Road, Darya Ganj, New Delhi-2, (ISBM- 8190461757), P- 109-110

Gupta, Nirmala (1989). Indian Adaptation of Career Maturity Inventory (CMI). Agra: National Psychological Corporation.

Hart, C. (1998). Doing a literature review. London: Sage.

Hewitt, L.S. (2006). "Age and sex differences in the career aspirations of elementary school children." Journal of Social Psychology, 96(2), 173-177.

Hochschild, J.L. (2003): social class in public schools. Journal of Social Issues, 59(4), 821-840.

Holland (1959): A Theory of Vocational Choice. Blaisdell Pychol. 6, 35-45.

Holland, J. L. (1959). A theory of vocational choice. Journal of Counselling Psychology, 6, pp. 35-44.

Holtan, T. C. (1962). 'Career Decision Making.' J. of Counsel. Psychol., 9, 291-299.

References

Indowu and Dere (2007). "Socio-economic status and occupational aspirations of High school Seniors in Nigeria." Journal of Educational Counselling, 20(4), 136-192.

Isaac, O.O. & Mopelola, O.A. (2014). Effects of Parental Influence on Adolescents' Career Choice in Badagry Local Government Area of Lagos State, Nigeria. IOSR Journal of Research & Method in Education (IOSR-JRME) e-ISSN: 2320–7388, p-ISSN: 2320–737X Volume 4, Issue 4 Ver. III (Jul-Aug. 2014), PP. 44-57 www.iosrjournals.org

Isaac, O.O., et.al. (2014). Effects of parental influence on Adolescents Career Choice in Badagry local Government Area of Lagos state, Nigeria, IOSR Journal of Research and Method in Education, vol. 4, issue 4, ver. 3, pp 44-57.

J. P. Banarjee, (2010). Education in India, Past, Present and future', Published by Amitav Roy, Central Library, 15/3, Shyama Charan Dey Street Kolkata-700073, P- 70

J. P. Banarjee, (2010). Education in India, Past, Present and future', Published by Amitav Roy, Central Library, 15/3, Shyama Charan Dey Street Kolkata-700073, P- 159

Jagannath, Mohanty (2002). 'Primary and Elementary Education (Policy and Programme, Growth and Development, Organization and Management, Sociological and Psychological Aspects, Democracy and Education)', Published by Deep andDeep Publication PVT. LTD. F-159 Rajouri Garden, New Delhi-110027 (ISBN-8176293725), P- 34

Jaggars, S. S. (2014) Choosing Between Online and Face-to-Face Courses: Community College Student Voices. American Journal of Distance Education.28(1)pages 27-38

Jahan, A. (2008). A Comparative Study of Frustration Among Under-Graduate Students in Relation to Their Value Profiles and Socio-Economic Background Variables. Department of Education AMU, Aligarh.

Johnson, Lourie (1995): A multidimensional analysis of the vocational aspirations of college students. Measurement and evaluation in counseling and development, vol. 28(1), 25-44.

Johnston ,S. and Barbour M. K. (2013).Measuring Success: Examining Achievement and Perceptions of Online Advanced Placement Students American Journal of Distance Education.27(1). pages 16-28

Juneja, A. and Rikhi, M. (2017). Influence of family environment and work values on vocational preference across career stages in young adults. IOSR Journal of Humanities and Social Sciences (IOSR-JHSS), vol. 22, Issue 10, ver. I, pp 82-91.

Kalia, A. K., & Sahu, S. (2013). A study of influence of type of school, SES and alienation on emotional adjustment of adolescents. Advanced International Research Journal of Teacher Education, 1(1), 13-19.

Kalita Utpal (2013). "Academic Performance in relation to Institutional Facilities and Career Expectations of Mishing students: A study" Ph.D. Thesis.

Kamala (1970). "Educational and Vocational Aspiration and Planning by High School Girls." Journal of Education and Psychology, XXVIII (3).

Kanna, V. & Rani, N. (2013). Vocational preferences of high school students in relation to their social intelligence. Conflux Journal of Education, 1(3), ISSN: 2320-9305

Kaur, V. (2014). Study the level of frustration among rural students in relation to occupational aspirations. An international peer reviewed and referred Scholarly research Journal for Interdisciplinary Studies, ISSN 2278-8808, PP. 2046-2051

Kentli, F.D. (2014). Perceived influences in vocational preferences of Turkish high school students. KEFAD, vol. 15, issue 2, 119-132.

Kerlinger, F.N. (1979). Behavioral Research: A conceptual approach, New York: Holt, Rinehart, and Winston.

References

Khan, N.S. and Jemberu, J. (2002). "Influence of SES on the Educational and Occupational Aspirations of High & Low Achieving Adolescents." Journal of Community Guidance and Research, Vol. 19, No. (1), pp. 113-118.

Khurshid, F., Tanvir, A., and Qasmi, N.F. (2012). Relationship between Study Habits and Academic Achievement among Hostel Living and Day Scholars' University Students. British Journal of Humanities and Social Sciences, Vol. 3 (2). ISSN 2048-1268. P. No.34-42.

Kitchenham, Barbara. Procedures for performing systematic reviews. Technical report TR/SE0401, Keele University, 2004.

Kochhar, S. K (1981). 'Pivotal Issues in Indian Education', Sterling Publishers Private Limited, New Delhi-110016, P- 14

Kochung, E. and Migunde, Q. (2011). Factors influencing students career choices among secondary school students in Kisumu Municipality, Kenya. JETERAPS, 2(2): 81-87.

Korkmaza, H. (2015). Factors Influencing Students' Career Chooses in Science and Technology: Implications for High School Science Curricula. Procedia - Social and Behavioral Sciences 197 (2015) 966 – 972, 7th World Conference on Educational Sciences, (WCES-2015), 05-07 February 2015, Novotel Athens Convention Center, Athens, Greece.

Koul, Lokesh (2009). Methodology of Educational Research (4th ed.) Vikash Publishing House Private Limited, New Delhi, p.317.

Krieger, N.; Williams, D.R. and Moss, N.E. (1997). Measuring social class in U.S. Public health research concept, methodologies and guidelines. Annual Review of Public Health, 18, 341-378.

Krishna, K.R. and Ansari, M.A. (1975). "Influence of personality factors, risk on occupational choices among college students." Journal of Psychological Research, 19(1), 32-40.

Kumar, L. S. and Bharat I. F.(2009) .Course Evaluation: A Holistic Approach Indian Journal of Open Learning 18(2).

Kumar, R. (2017). A comparative Study of Vocational Interests of Secondary School Students in Relation to Their Gender. Imperial Journal of Interdisciplinary Research (IJIR), Imperial Journal of Interdisciplinary Research (IJIR) Vol-3, Issue-4, 2017 ISSN: 2454-1362, http://www.onlinejournal.in

Kumar, R. (2017). A Comparative Study of Vocational Interests of Secondary School Students in Relation to Their Gender. Imperial Journal of Interdisciplinary Research (IJIR) Vol-3, Issue-4, 2017 ISSN: 2454-1362. p. no. 1177-1180.

Kumari, V. R. S.; Chamundeswari, S. (2015). Achievement Motivation, Study Habits and Academic Achievement of Students at the Secondary Level. IJERMT. ISSN-2278-9359, Vol. 4, issue- 10. Pp. 7-13.

Kuppuswamy, B. (1960). An analysis of some variable involved in socio-economic variable. Journal of Education and Psychology, 18.

Kuruba, G. (2008). Adoption of New Technologies - An Intervention in the Development of ODL in Botswana. Indian Journal of Open Learning 17, (2).

Kuruba, G. (1999) Distance Education in Developing Countries A Case of Botswana. Indian Journal of Open Learning 8(1).

Ladany et al. (19997). "At Risk Urban High School Students Commitment to Career Choices." Journal of Counselling and Development, Vol. 76.

Maccuish, D. A. (2004). Evaluation in Distance Learning: Fluff or Substance. Indian Journal of Open Learning. 13 (1).

Machi, L.E. and B.T. McEvoy (2009). The Literature Review: Six Steps to Success. Thousand Oaks: Corwin Sage.

Mahak, Mera (1999). "Adolescents' Vocational Aspirations and Economic Status of the Family." The Progress of Education, Vol. LXXIII, No .10, May.

Mahanta, Kashyap and Khataniar, Guruprasad (2014). "Distance Learning in India: A comparative study", the clarion. Vol.3, no.2, pp 75-82.

Mahmood, Azhar; Mahmood, Sheikh, Tariq; Malik, Allah Bakhsh (2012). A comparative study of student satisfaction level in Distance Learning and Live classroom at Higher Education Level, Turkish online Journal of Distance Education, V13n1, p128-136, Jan 2012)

Majoribanks, Alvin, S.R. (2008). "School Attitudes and adolescents aspirations ethnic group differences." International Journal of Psychology, 23(3), 277-289.

Malik, N. A, Belawati, T. and Baggaley, J.P (2005) Framework of Collaborative Research and Development on Distance Learning Technology in Asia. Indian Journal of Open Learning 14, (3).

Mangal, S. K. and Mangal, Uma (2009) Essential of Educational Technology PHI Learning Pvt. Ltd., New Delhi.

Mangal, S.K., (1993). Advanced Educational Psychology, Prentice Hall, New Delhi, India. **241**

Manjulika, S. Reddy ,V. V and, Fulzele ,F. (1996).Student Opinion of Counselling : The Experience of Indira Gandhi National Open University. Indian Journal of Open Learning .5(2).

Mann, Prem, S. (1995). Introductory Statistics (2nd ed.). Wiley. ISBN 0-471-31009-3.

Mark M. H. and Hillx W.A.: Systems and Theories in Psychology, New Delhi, Tata McGraw Hill Publishing Co, 1973.

Mathur, Purnima and Gaur, J.S. (1984). "The Effect of SES on the level of occupational aspiration of the higher secondary school students in Delhi." An Investigation," Manas, 21(2), 43-51.

Mathur, S.S., (2008). Development of Learner and Teaching Learning Process, Agrawal Publication, Agra.

Mattoo, M.I. (2013). Career Choices of Secondary Students with Special Reference to Gender, Type of Stream and Parental Education. Research on Humanities and Social Sciences www.iiste.org ISSN 2222-1719 (Paper), ISSN 2222-2863 (Online), Vol.3, No.20,

Mattoo, M.I. (2013). Career choices of secondary students with special reference to gender, type of stream and parental education. Research on humanities and social sciences, vol. 3, no. 20.

Maurice, Waite (ed. 1994) The Little Oxford Dictionary of Current English, (Delhi: Oxford University Press, 1994), pi28.

Mc Laughlin, Gerald, W. et al. (1976). "Socio-economic status and the career aspirations and perceptions of women seniors in High Schools." Vocational Guidance Quarterly, 25(2), 155-162.

Mcneal JR, R. B. (2012) Online Versus Traditional Instruction: Quasi-Experimental Evidence from a College-Level Introduction to Sociology Course. Indian Journal of Open Learning 21(1).

Medupin, C. (2012) Women and Environment through Distance Education. International Women Online Journal of Distance Education,.1(3).

Mehta, Mathur, et.al. (1987). Influences of level of vocational aspirations of adolescents. Indian educational review, 42-60.

Mehta, P.K and Saxena ,A. (2004) .Emerging Trends in Student Assessment in ODLS. Indian Journal of Open Learning.13 (2).

Menon M. B. (1998) Open Learning and Distance Education in India- An Introspection. Indian Journal of Open Learning 7(3).

Metha, H. Perin et al. (1987). "Influence of occupational aspiration of Adolescents." Indian Educational Review, A research Journal of NCERT, Vol. 22, No. 3, p. 42.

Miller, I.W. and Haller, A.O. (1964). "A measure of level of occupational aspiration." Personal and guidance journal, 42, 448-455.

Mirowsky J, Ross CE,(1998). Education, personal control, lifestyle and Health - a human capital hypothesis. Research on Aging; 20 : 415–49.

Mirza, J.S(1997). On Mixing Delivery Modes of Conventional and Distance Education : A Pragmatic View. Indian Journal of Open Learning 6(1-2)

Mishra, S. and Gaba, A.K. (2001).How do Distance Learners Use Activities in Self-Instructional Materials? Indian Journal of Open Learning. 10(1).

Misra, Satayanarayana & Monalisa, Bal (1988). Growth, development and elitism: an insight into commissions on higher education.

Mohan, V. & Vohra, H.B.L. (1981). An investigation of patterns of vocational choices of polytechnic students. Indian Journal of Technical Education, vol. 7(1), 16-22.

Mohsin, S.M. And Hussain, S. (1970). Manual for Mohsin, Shamshad Hindi Adaptation of Bell Adjustment Inventory, Mahendru : Patna. Psycho-Scientific Works, Publication Division.

Mona & Kaur, J. (2008). "Career Maturity of Adolescents in Relation to Intelligence."

Monika, et al. (2014). A study of vocational interest of male and female sports students of university. Research Journal of Physical Education Sciences, vol. 2(6), 8-12.

Monika, Santosh & Sushil, L. (2014). A Study of Vocational Interest of Male and Female Sports Students of University. Research Journal of Physical Education Sciences, ISSN 2320– 9011, 2(6), pp. 8-12

Moodley, S. (2002) Inclusive Education: Challenges for Distance Learning, Policy and Practice Pathway 6 Conference 2002.

Moore, M. G. 1972. Learner autonomy: The second dimension of independent learning. Convergence Fall:76-88.

Moore, M. G. 1994. Autonomy and interdependence. The American Journal of Distance Education 8 (2): 15

Moore, M.G. ed. (2013). Handbook of distance education. Routledge.

Morgan, C.T. (1961). 'Introduction to Psychology and Education'. NY McGraw-Hill.

Mouly G.J: Psychology for Effective Teaching, H.O.H. Rinehart and Winston Inc. New York, 1973, 85-86.

Mulay, V. (1986)."Correspondence Education in Indian University-A Review." Report of the Project Team, University Grants Commission.

Mullick, S.P. (1995)Emergence of Distance Education Professionals in India: A Profile of the First Cohort M.A.3 in Distance Education. Indian Journal of Open Learning 4(1).

Musaiger, A.O. (2005). Lifestyle Factors Associated with obesity Among Male University Students in the United Arab Emirates, Journal Nutrition and Food Science, 33(4): 145-147.

NAAC.gov.in/aboutus.asp

Nadeem, N.A. & Ahmad, Ishfaq. (2016). Career Preferences of Male and Female Higher Secondary Students – A Comparative study. International Journal of Scientific, 4(2), pp. 4973-4982, ISSN: 2321-7545

Nadeem, N.A. and Ahmad, I. (2016). Career Preferences of male and female Higher Secondary students- A Comparative study. International Journal of Scientific Research and Education, vol. 4, issue 2, pp 4973-4982.

Nagar, Rashmi (1991). "A study of vocational aspiration of educated girls in Gorakhpur Division and Facilities available to them. Ph.D. Thesis Published.

Naidu, C.G. (1994). Social Demands and Educational Planning in Distance Education. Paper presented at the Indian Education Association Conference on Increasing Access to Distance Education: An Agenda for Action. Tirupati.

Naik, J. P. (1982). The education commission and after. APH Publishing.

Naoshi, Maeuezato (2003). Study on Lifestyle of University Students—Views on Health and Health Behaviors, Journal of Hokkaido University of Education, Japan, 53(2), 73-79.

Natalie (2006). "Factors influencing career choice of Adolescents and Young Adults in Rural Pennsylvania." Extension Journal, Vol. 44, No. 3.

Nathan (2004), "Academic Performance, Career Potential, Creativity, and job performance: can one construct predict then all." Journal of Personality and Social Psychology, Vol. 86, No. 1, 148-161.

Nautiyal, Rashmi & Abraham, A. (2002). A Study of Values of Undergraduate and Postgraduate Students as Determinant of their Vocational Preferences, Unpublished Ph.D Thesis, Dr. B. R. Ambedkar University, Agra.

Nembiakkim Rose and Mishra Sanjaya (2010). Distance Education Research: Attitudes and Barriers . Indian Journal of Open Learning, 2010, 19(3), 215-222

Ninghtoujam, Niakumari (1987). Study Culture among University Students, University News, 35(52), 10-15.

Numan, A.; Hasan, S. S. (2017). Effect of Study Habits on Test Anxiety and Academic Achievement of Undergraduate Students. Journal of Research and Reflections in Education. Vol. 11, No 1, pp. 1-14.

Nuthana, P & Yenagi, G. (2009). Influence of study habits, self-concept on academic achievement of boys and girls. Karnataka J. Agric. Sci., 22 (5) (1135-1138).

O' Brien, Karen M. & Fissinger, Ruth E. (1993). A causal model of the career orientation and career choice of adolescent women. Journal of Counseling Psychology, Vol 40(4), 456-469.

O'Brien, Karen M., & Fassinger, Ruth E. (1993). A casual model of the career orientation and career choice of adolescent women. Journal of counseling psychology, vol. 40(4), 456-469.

Ogunleye, A. (2013) Quality Assurance and Quality Indicators in Open and Distance Education: Context, Concerns and Challenges. International Journal of Educational Research and Technology, 4(2) 49-62.

Olakulehin, F. K. and Ojo, O. D. (2006). Distance Education as a Women Empowerment Strategy in Africa. Indian Journal of Open Learning 15(3).

Olamide, S.O. & Olawaiye, S.O. (2013). The Factors Determining the Choice of Career Among Secondary School Students. The International Journal of Engineering and Science (IJES), 2(6), pp. 33-44, ISSN(e): 2319 – 1813 ISSN(p): 2319 – 1805

Olugbenga, D. O. Olakulehin, F. K.. Remi and others (2007). Evaluation of Assessment Methods as Correlates of Quality Assurance and Certification Standard in ODL Institutions. Indian Journal of Open Learning 16(3).

Oluwatimilehin, J. and Owoyele, J. (2012). Study Habits and Academic Achievement in Core Subjects Among Junior Secondary School Students in Ondo State, Nigeria. Bulgarian Journal of Science and Education Policy (BJSEP), Vol. 6 (1). P. No.155- 169.

Ory, J.C. and Helfrick, L.M. (2002). "A study of Individual Characteristics and Career Aspirations." Vocational Guidance Quarterly, 27(1), 43-49.

Osei, C.K. and Mensah, J.A., (2011). A comparative study of student Academic Performance in on-campus Teaching and Distance Learning in a Computer Engineering Programme, Journal of Science and Technology, Vol. 31, No. 1 (2011), PP 97)

Otta, F.E. & William, N.O. (2012). Self-concept and vocational interest among secondary school students (adolescents). Asian Journal of Social Sciences & Humanities, ISSN: 2186-8492, ISSN: 2186-8484 Print Vol. 1. No. 4. November 2012

Otta, F.E. et.al. (2012). Self-concept and vocational interest among secondary school students (adolescents), ISSN: 2186-8492, vol. 1, no. 4.

Oztuna D, Elhan AH, Tuccar E. (2006). Investigation of four different normality tests in terms of type 1 error rate and power under different distributions. Turkish Journal of Medical Sciences. 2006;36(3):171–6.

Paliwal, R. R. (2004) Linguistic Plurality and Distance Education in India: A Perspective. Indian Journal of Open Learning.13 (2).

Palos, R. and Drobot, L. (2010). The impact of family influence on the career choice of adolescents. Procedia Social and Behavioral Sciences.

Paloú, R. & Drobot, L. (2010). The impact of family influence on the career choice of adolescents. Procedia Social and Behavioral Sciences, 2 (2010) 3407–3411

Panda, B.N., (2007). Advanced Educational Psychology, Discovery Publishing House, New Delhi

Panda, S. (2005) Higher Education at a distance and national development. Journal of Distance Education .26(2)

Panda, S. (2011). Distance Education in International Contexts: Planning and Management Imperatives. Indian Journal of Open Learning. 20(1).

Panda, S., Venkaiah, V. and Garg, S. (2006). Tracing the historical development in open and distance education. Puranik and S.Panda .(Eds) Four Decades of Distance Education in India Reflections on Policy and Practice, Viva Book Pvt. Ltd., (pp. 3-33) New Delhi.

Pareek, U. and Trivedi, G. (1964). Categorization of rural socio-economic group. Journal of social Work, 24, 293-303.

Parsons, Frank (1967). Choosing a vocation, New York L Agathon Press, Inc.

Parveen, A (2013). Personality Traits, Study Habits and Educational Aspirations of Secondary School Muslim Students in Relation to Their Academic Achievement. Department of Education AMU, Aligarh.

Parveen, D. (2014). Career preference, self-esteem, intelligence and socioeconomic status as determinants of academic achievement at the secondary school level. Ph.D. thesis. Department of Education. AMU. Aligarh.

Passt, B.K. (1970). "Patterns of vocational aspirations of higher secondary school adolescents in relation to sex and residential background." Journal of education and psychology. Vol. XXVIII (20), 57-65.

Pathak & Rahman (2013). A study on the career preferences of undergraduate students in relation to their sex, rural, urban inhabitation and level of media exposure. International Journal of Humanities and Social Science.

Perraton, H. 1988. A theory for distance education. In Distance education: International perspectives, ed. D. Sewart, D. Keegan, and B. Holmberg, 34-45. New York: Routledge

Peter, S. (2008). Lifestyle of Hungarian Adolescents—Observations among Metropolitan Secondary school students, Annals of Nutrition and Metabolism, 52(2). **242**

Peters, 0. 1988. Distance teaching and industrial production: A comparative interpretation in outline. In Distance education: International perspectives, ed. D. Sewart, D. Keegan, and B. Holmberg, 95113. New York: Routledge.

Peters, O. (1994). distance education and industrial production: A comparative interpretation in outline (1973). Otto Peters on distance education: the industrialisation of teaching and learning, 107-127.

Pike, G.R. (2006). Vocational preferences and college expectations: an extension of Holland's principal of selection. Research in Higher Education, 47(5). Pp. 591-612

Pike, G.R. (2006). Vocational Preferences and college expectations: An extension of Holland's Principle of Self Selection. Research in Higher Education, vol. 47, no. 5.

Piko, B. and Fitzpatrick, K. M. (2001). Does class matter ? SES and Psychological health among Hungarian adolescents. Social Science Medicine, 53, 817-830.

Poonam, Aashim and Kaur, P. (2011). "Career choices and academic achievement of secondary school students". Indian Journal of Psychometry and Education, 42(1): 91-93.

Powers, M.G. (1981). Measures of socio-economic status : An Introduction, In M.G. Powers (Ed.), Measures of socio-economic status : current issues Boulder, CO : Westview.

Prasad ,N. (2004) Programme Evaluation Under Open Learning System: An Evaluation of CLD Programme of IGNOU Indian Journal of Open Learning. 13(3).

Prospectus (2012). Directorate of Distance Education, Vidyasagar University, Prospectus for M.A from July 2012. Netaji Subhas Open University, Kolkata

Prospectus, (2012). Directorate of Distance Education, Rabindra Bharati University, Kolkata .

Puju, J. A. & Khan, M. A. (2019). Self-concept and study habits of visually impaired and hearing impaired college going students. Volume-04 ISSN: 2455-3085 (Online) Issue-02 RESEARCH REVIEW International Journal of Multidisciplinary February-2019 www.rrjournals.com[UGC Listed Journal], pp. 352-356

Pulkkinen L. (1992), Life-styles in personality development. Special Issue : Longitudinal research and personality. European Journal of Personality; 6:139–55.

Raddy, R. G. (1985) Dr. B.R. Ambedkar Open University: It's Role in Higher Education, International seminar of Distance Education.

Raina, R. & Bhargava, R. (2002). Students morale and career achievement. Psycho-lingua, 32(1), 49-52.

Rana, S. and Kausar, R (2011). Comparison of Study Habits and Academic Performance of Pakistani British and White British Students. Pakistan Journal of Social and Clinical Psychology, Vol. 9, 21-26.

Razia, B and Ahmad, N. (2017). Emotional Intelligence and Socio-Economic Status as the Determinants of Academic Achievement Among Adolescents. International Journal of Education and Psychological Research. Vol. 6, Issue 2, 2017.

Roe, Anne (1956). The psychology of occupations. New York: John Willey and Sons.

Rosenberg, M. (1957). Occupation and values. Glencoe, Illinois: Free Press.

Sahu, S. (2012). Alienation, career maturity and study habits of adolescents in relation to academic achievement, locus of control and socio-economic status. Doctoral thesis (Edu), Maharishi Dayanand University, Rohtak, Haryana.

Sharma, D. K (2016International Journal of Science and Research (IJSR) ISSN (Online): 2319-7064 Index Copernicus Value (2013): 6.14

Singh, P. & Choudhary, G. (2015). Understanding frustration level among adolescents in relation to their socio-economic status- an analytical study. ZENITH International Journal of Multidisciplinary Research, ISSN 2231-5780 Vol.5 (3), pp. 165-174 Online available at zenithresearch.org.in

Singh, P. and Choudhary, G. (2015). Understanding Frustration among Adolescents in Relation to their Socio-Economic Status-An Analytical Study. ZENITH International Journal of Multidisciplinary Research. ISSN 2231-5780 Vol.5 (3), pp. 165-174.

Singh, Y. G. (2011). Academic Achievement and Study Habits of Higher Secondary Students. International Referred Research Journal. ISSN-0975-3486, Vol-III, Issue-27, pp.19-20.

Tiedman, D. G., O' Hara, R. P. (1956) Career Development: Choice and Adjustment., Prentice Hall.

Tiedman, D. V. & Pandit, J. L. (1958). On identity and level of occupational aspirations, unpublished manuscript, Harvard studies in career development. Harvard University.

University Grant Commission, New Delhi (2006). Higher education in India. Emerging issues related to access, inclusiveness and quality www.ugc.ac.in/oldpdf/chair_sdt/chairman_nehru_lecture.pdf

Upreti, H.C. and N. Upreti (1984). College girls on choosing a career in social welfare, vol. 31(2), 9-11.

Vandse, U.S. and Poll, S.A. (1990). Look Back-Look Forward: A Survey of Distance Learners, Bombay. SNDT Women's University.

Vandse,U. (1988) Problems of Women Learners in Distance Education. Women In Distance Education- Issues & Prospects. WIN and ICDE.

Varghese, N. V. (2009). Globalization, the Current Economic Crisis and Higher Education Development, Journal of Educational Planning and Administration (XXIII) 3, July 2009.

Venkaiah, V. and Mouli, C. R. (2003) Open Distance Learning in Andhra Pradesh. Indian Journal of Open Learning , 12(3).

Verma E. and Bakhshi R. (2017). Career Preferences and Academic Performance: A Gender Based Study. International Journal of Advanced Education and Research ISSN: 2455-5746, Volume 2; Issue 3; May 2017; Page No. 200-203.

Verma, E. & Bakshi, R. (20170. Career preferences and academic performance: A gender-based study. International Journal of Advanced Education and Research, 2(3), pp. 200-203, ISSN: 2455-5746

Verma, E. and Bakshi, R. (2017). Career Preferences and academic performance: A gender based study. International Journal of Advanced Education and Research, Vol.2, Issue 3, pp 200-203.

Villi ,C. (2003). Study on Knowledge, Attitude Perception and Expectations (KAPE) of the Women Learners of Open University. Indian Journal of Open Learning .12(1-2).

Vlachopoulou, M. Manos, B. and Chrysopoulou, S. (2005)Methodological Approaches for Blended Learning Evaluation. Indian Journal of Open Learning, 14 (3).

Volk, J.H., Rashid, A.T. and Elder, L. (2010). Using Mobile Phones to Improve Educational Outcomes: An Analysis of Evidence from Asia. The International Review of Research in Open and Distance Learning, 11(1). Athabasca University Press, Canada.

Vunnam, V. and Salawu, I. O. (2009) .Student Attrition in Dr. B.R. Ambedkar Open University. Indian Journal of Open Learning 18(3).

Vyas, S & Choudhary, G. (2017). Relationship of socio-economic status with frustration, self-concept, study habits and academic achievement of adolescents. International Journal of Advanced Research and Development, ISSN: 2455-4030, www.advancedjournal.com, Volume 2; Issue 3; pp. 46-51

Vyas, S. and, Choudhary, G. (2017). Relationship of Socio-Economic Status with Frustration, Self-Concept, Study Habits and Academic Achievement of Adolescents. International Journal of Advanced Research and Development ISSN: 2455-4030, Volume 2; Issue 3; May 2017; Page No. 46-51.

Warren, H.C. (1934). Dictionary of Psychology. London: George Allen and Unwin. Ltd.

Webster, Jane and Watson, Richard T. (2002). Analyzing the past to prepare for the future: Writing a literature review. MIS Quarterly, 26(2).

Wedemeyer, C.A. (1971). Independent study. The encyclopedia of education, 4, 548-557.

Wengrowicz N.and Offir, B. (2013)Teachers' Perceptions of Transactional Distance in Different Teaching Environments. American Journal of Distance Education 27(2) p.p 111-121

West R. E. (2011) Insights From Research on Distance Education Learners, Learning, and Learner Support. American Journal of Distance Education 25(3) p.p135-151

Westaway, Margart and Skuy, M. (2009). "Self Esteem and the Educational and Vocational Aspirations of Adolescent Girls in South Africa." South African Journal of Psychology, 124(4), 113-117.

White, Karl R. (1982). The Relation between socio-economic status (SES) and academic achievement. Psychological Bulletin Vol. 91 (3) 461-481 doi 10.1037/0033-2909.913 461.

Williams, A.P. and Woodward, S. (1990). "Factors related to career aspirations of new entrants into a stratified occupational system." British Journal of Guidance and Counselling, 11(1), 68-81.

Woolfolk, Anita and Wayne K. H. (1990). Prospective teacher's sense of efficacy and beliefs about control. Journal of educational psychology, 82(1), 81.

Wu, W.T. (2000). Vocational Interests and Career Maturity of Male High School Students Talented in Math and Science. Proc. Natl. Sci. Counc. ROC(D), 10(3), PP. 137-143

Yadav, A. (1993) Learning System: A Model for Conceptual Analysis. Indian Journal of Open Learning. 2(2).

Yadav, R. (2000). "The Vocational Preferences of Adolescents in Relation to their Intelligence and Achievement." Journal of Educational Research and Extension, Vol. 37, No. 3, pp. 36-45.

Zahra, W. (2016). A Study of Vocational Interests of Adolescents on the Basis of Educational Boards. Acme Intellects International Journal of Research in Management, Social Sciences & Technology ISSN 2320 – 2939 (Print) 2320-2793 (Online), 13(13), pp. 1-12.

Zara, S.S. (2010). "Effects of learning styles on career preferences of senior secondary school students in Jigawa State, Nigeria." Eds. Journal of Counselling, Vol. 3, No. 1.

Zunker, Venon G. (1994). Career counseling- applied concepts of life planning. California: Brooks/Cole Publishing Co.

www.ingramcontent.com/pod-product-compliance
Lightning Source LLC
LaVergne TN
LVHW020448070526
838199LV00063B/4886